The
Best Shots
You've
Never
Tried

Avon, Massachusetts

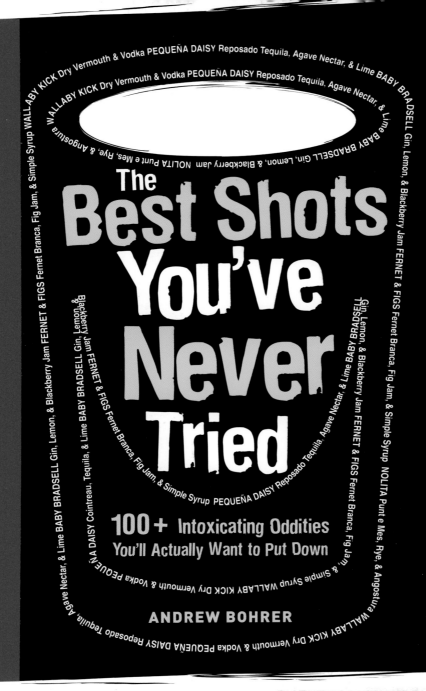

The Best Shots You've Never Tried

100+ Intoxicating Oddities
You'll Actually Want to Put Down

ANDREW BOHRER

Published by
Adams Media, a division of F+W Media, Inc.
57 Littlefield Street, Avon, MA 02322. U.S.A.
www.adamsmedia.com

ISBN 10: 1-4405-3617-1
ISBN 13: 978-1-4405-3617-5
eISBN 10: 1-4405-3879-4
eISBN 13: 978-1-4405-3879-7

Printed in China.

10   9   8   7   6   5   4   3   2   1

This publication is designed to provide accurate and authoritative information with regard to the subject matter covered. It is sold with the understanding that the publisher is not engaged in rendering legal, accounting, or other professional advice. If legal advice or other expert assistance is required, the services of a competent professional person should be sought.
—From a *Declaration of Principles* jointly adopted by a Committee of the American Bar Association and a Committee of Publishers and Associations

Many of the designations used by manufacturers and sellers to distinguish their product are claimed as trademarks. Where those designations appear in this book and Adams Media was aware of a trademark claim, the designations have been printed with initial capital letters.

These recipes were created for adults age 21 and older, and are not intended to promote the excessive consumption of alcohol. Alcohol, when consumed to excess, can directly or indirectly result in permanent injury or death. The author, Adams Media, and F+W Media, Inc. do not accept liability for any injury, loss, legal consequence, or incidental or consequential damage incurred by reliance on the information provided in this book.

This book is available at quantity discounts for bulk purchases.
For information, please call 1-800-289-0963.

Dedication

To Michelle Broderick, you have no pants,
but I still love you forever

CONTENTS

Part 3:
FARMERS' MARKET 82

Part 4:
HOLIDAYS. 122

Part 5:
DESSERT & AFTER DINNER......154

Part 6:
SHOTS OF LAST RESORT 200

Index 232

Introduction

The introduction to hard liquor for most people is the shot. Frequently that involves doing continuous shots of gin until Dad's bottle is empty. During college years, tequila often mysteriously becomes animated and will, all by itself, shoot down the throats of young people. Many of tequila's victims never forgive it for this trespass. However, shots, if taken in tiny portions to toast, commemorate, or mourn, can take on an all new purpose. The unique shots in this book will show you that just the right amount is enough to make a memory, not lose a memory.

A doctor will give shots to maintain health and ward off illness. The drinking culture needs a shot too. The shot is often maligned as a drunk's drink: a way of drinking that is not about enjoyment. Though that can often be true, shots are also about ritual, togetherness, and the creation of memories. They also don't need to be boring. Many of the ensuing shots will address experimentation and learning new flavor combinations, so you can easily create delicious shots you've never tried before. You'll even find some shots of last resort that you can make in times of need just by using ingredients you have on hand.

WHAT YOU'LL NEED

Ice will be used in almost every shot you'll be mixing up. Rule number one about ice is that you need twice as much as you think. You can never reuse the same ice for a second set of drinks, and you always have to fill the shaker completely with ice. One ice tray in the fridge is good for about two rounds of drinks. Buy about 1 bag for every 15 guests you have. And you know that worthless friend who always shows up late and never knows what to bring? That guy needs to leave the onion dip and bag of chips at home. Tell him to bring ice.

Most homes have the correct tools to make cocktails, but people use them wrong. The worst culprits are the three-piece shaker or cobbler shaker and the muddler—just throw them out. You need a two-piece shaker or a Boston shaker. These consist of a metal tin and a pint glass and are much easier to use. The pint glass half will double as a mixing glass for stirred drinks. To stir drinks, you'll need a bar spoon (in a pinch, a chopstick does fine). A sharp knife prepares fruit and keeps enemies at bay. Buy a standard juice press from the green grocer. You'll need a hawthorne strainer (you know, the one with springs) and—to make shots a bit cleaner—a fine mesh strainer (also available at the grocer). And the most important tool is the measuring cup or jigger. This book will do the math for you, but you have to measure to make good drinks.

TECHNIQUE

Technique is easy. If a recipe has juice, cream, or fruit in it, shake it. Shake it as hard as you can for about 8 seconds. If a recipe is all alcohol or you can see through it, stir it. Stirring should go on for about 12 seconds. Building a shot in the glass will happen for pousse-cafés. For these shots, you'll pour each chilled spirit (keep them in the fridge) right into the glass, slowly layering them on top of each other to make a layered shot. A bar spoon works well to slow the flow of booze, but so does just pouring each spirit over a cherry held by the stem. Lastly, the fine mesh strainer is the shot's best friend; it keeps the little ice shards out. If you are having a hard time fine straining each little shot, try quickly straining out the entire cocktail into a separate glass. Then you can just pour from there.

Part 1

MINIATURE CLASSICS

We call them Classics for a reason. Miniature Classics are flavor combinations that have worked for a couple hundred years or so. Though they number into the thousands, they can be quite simple to remember. The Classics are really only six or seven cocktails, and ingredients are swapped out to make new drinks. Miniature Classics are the puppy dog version of their true breed. The flavors stay the same but are sweetened up and made cuter. It would not be inappropriate to glue little googly eyes on to these baby shots to increase their cuteness.

NoLita

Shooting Manhattans is great for forgetting a terrible evening but not great for staying awake. Every bartender knows, "If you drink to forget, pay your tab in advance." Named for the part of Manhattan North of Little Italy (get it?), the NoLita can be considered a reverse Manhattan. It is a gentle vermouth-ed whiskey shot. Adding more Punt e Mes, or a "point and a half," for a point of sweetness and a half of bitterness, will sweeten this drink even more. Stir this shot up to make it ice cold and enjoy the sweet herbal flavor of Italy and the spicy belligerence of American rye whiskey.

MAKES

1 ounce Punt e Mes

.5 ounce rye whiskey

2 dashes Angostura bitters

1. Stir and strain into a shot glass.

Angostura Bitters:
You Have a Bottle in Your House and You Don't Know Why

That little brown bottle lazily wrapped in a white label with a yellow cap is called Angostura bitters. It's the oldest commercially available bitters, and it has become so synonymous with bitters that some folks think it's the only one. In the modern world, it is just one of hundreds of bitters on the market, but Angostura's spicy clove and ginger flavor has been essential for cocktails for almost 200 years.

Little Lady

The Little Lady is a miniature version of the classic White Lady cocktail. Ordering a White Lady often makes people giggle depending on their proximity to the suburbs. When made correctly, the White Lady is a sublimely balanced cocktail tantamount to getting drunk on sunshine. You might notice that this shot is similar to a Sidecar or a Whiskey Sour but with gin. That is because it is the same drink: The 2 parts booze to 1 part sour to 1 part sweet is the cocktail template called a sour. However, the Little Lady is the most elegant sour.

MAKES

.75 ounce London dry gin

.5 ounce triple sec

.5 ounce lemon juice

1. Shake and strain into a shot glass.

The White Lady: *A Haunting Ghost*

In literature, the white lady refers to a white specter that is an omen for death. Though stories of this cocktail's origin vary widely, the White Lady cocktail is enjoyed by all and is a long time favorite of the men. Every time it's ordered, most bartenders try to hold back their laughter; the White Lady haunts its fans with the gibes of bartenders.

Friendship Test

Drinking to apathy is what the Friendship Test is all about. The inspiration for this shot is the ever-raging argument about who invented the Pisco Sour. Peruvians and Chileans both claim the grape brandy called pisco as their national booze and the Pisco Sour as their national cocktail. The only solution to this debate is to make tiny Pisco Sour shots until neither country cares anymore. Make round one from Peru and round two from Chile; keep repeating until no one is fighting.

MAKES

1 ounce pisco

.25 ounce lemon juice

.25 ounce simple syrup

1 egg white

Dash Angostura bitters

1. Shake first four ingredients very hard and strain into two shot glasses.

2. Drop a little dash of Angostura bitters atop the finished shot.

Chile vs. Peru: *Whose Pisco Is Better?*

The average person on the street in Peru or Chile can no sooner tell you the difference between each other's pisco than the average American knows the difference between bourbon whiskey and Scotch whiskey. In Peru, pisco is made in a pot still, distilled to proof, and un-aged; it is very similar to grappa. In Chile, pisco is made in a column still and aged in wood; it is similar to a very light cognac. These two countries couldn't make a more different product.

Piña de la Piña

The Piña Colada's mix of rum, pineapple, and coconut makes it the ultimate relaxation drink. A blended Piña Colada, especially when fresh, says to the world, "I am done; this frosty prize I have in my hand is the most important thing I'll do all day." So why not have it in shot form too? This is a much lighter version bereft of cream and crushed ice.

MAKES

1 ounce coconut water

1 ounce light rum

.5 ounce pineapple gomme syrup

1 lime wedge

1. Shake and strain first three ingredients into a shot glass. Put a lime wedge on the glass.

Pineapple Gomme Syrup:
How to Say It, Why You Use It, and How to Make It

Well, the first part is easy: "Gum." And it is used in place of canned pineapple, which is mostly juice sugar, and freshly squeezed pineapple juice, which can be quite acidic. Pineapple gomme syrup gives you the freshness and the aroma without having to manage big spiky fruits or diabetes-inducing canned corn syrup preserves. To make pineapple gomme syrup, take one cored pineapple (preferably fresh and ripe), soak it in thirty-two ounces of water overnight. This will give you lightly sweetened and acidic pineapple-ish water. To make it into syrup just dissolve in sugar to taste, about 2 cups over light heat should do the trick.

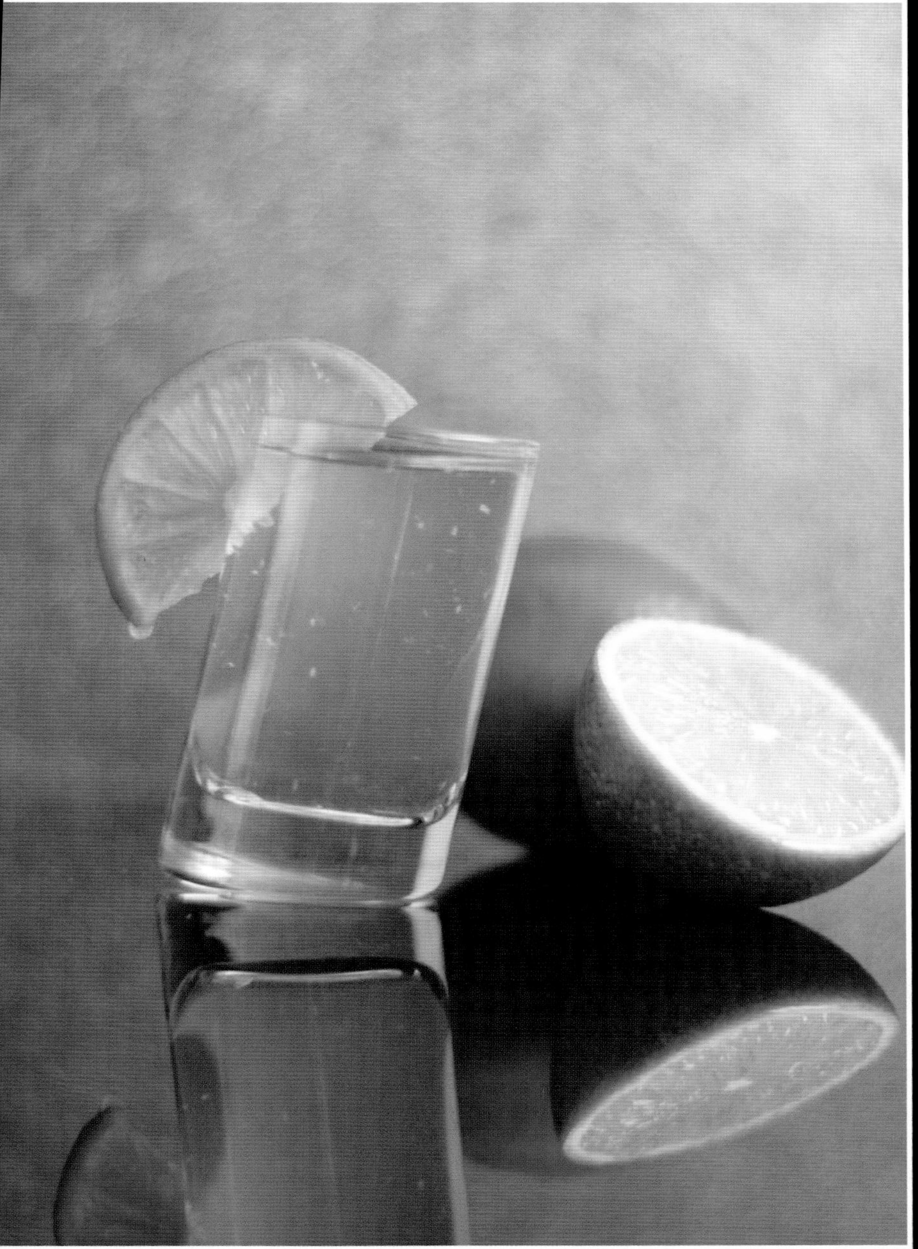

Declarative

Some people write like Dickens. Those people are paid by the word. Others write like Hemingway. Those people are brief. The Declarative shot is inspired by the Hemmingway Daiquiri and is named for his use of declarative sentences. His drinking matched his writing style: intense and specific. The Hemingway Daiquiri combined grapefruit, maraschino, rum, and lime. It is less sweet than what you are used to.

MAKES

1 ounce light rum

.5 ounce maraschino liqueur

.5 ounce grapefruit juice

2 dashes Peychaud's bitters

1. Shake and strain the first three ingredients into a shot glass.
2. Top the shot with 2 dashes of Peychaud's bitters and a short declarative sentence.

Maraschino: *It Isn't What You Think It Is*

Maraschino is a bittersweet and dry liqueur originating in Dalmatia Croatia. It is made from marasca cherries and their crushed cherry pits. It tastes lightly of a cherry-scented, swampy locker room but in a good way.

Peychaud's Bitters:

Best Known as "The Other Kind of Bitters"

The second most common bottle of bitters is the one invented by Antoine Amédée Peychaud back in 1830. It is the essential ingredient in several classic cocktails, most notably the Sazerac. Unlike almost all bitters, Peychaud's dry out cocktails with a light anise flavor.

Paul's #8 Boutique

When you drink rum, you want to feel like an explorer, a pirate, or Jimmy Buffet. For Buffet, you want a crisp daiquiri or something in a pineapple as you wear a floral shirt. As a pirate, you just want more rum and a jaunty song. But rum is best when it takes you to some crazy exotic flavor, which is the voyage that Paul's #8 Boutique will take you on. This shot's name is inspired by the falernum pioneer Paul Clarke, and it is a miniature version of the awful-sounding Corn n' Oil cocktail. Falernum is a rum-based, lime-spiced liqueur. Paul's #8 Boutique will carry you to an unknown port in the Caribbean and a bar with talking parrots and ex-pats from the globe over.

MAKES

.75 ounce aged rum

.75 ounce falernum

1 dash Angostura bitters

.25 ounce lime juice

1. Shake and strain into a shot glass.

Navigating the Seas of Rum:
What Is Dark Rum?

Dark rum refers to any rum that is not light. This could mean that the rum has been aged or artificially colored. When shopping for a dark rum, look for some sort of indicator of age (e.g., a number of years aged). If you can't find one, put it back on the shelf and get something that tastes rich. Jamaican and Guatemalan rums will generally have the full flavor you need.

Wintour

Severe, delicate, refined, and misunderstood—named after the equally feared and respected chief editor of Vogue magazine, Anna Wintour, the Wintour shot also draws its inspiration from the classic cocktail the White Spider. The shot is not thusly named to put Anna in any sort of arachnid family; rather it is an attempt to better explain a classic. By all accounts, the classic White Spider tastes of a hideously boozy Girl Scout cookie gone wrong. The Wintour shot aims to add subtlety and nuance to maligned and misused ingredients. The culprits called crème de menthe and crème de cacao ruin many a cocktail, but not here. The Wintour shot is classic and timeless.

MAKES

1 ounce vodka

.25 ounce clear crème de menthe

.25 ounce clear crème de cacao

1. Shake and strain into a shot glass.

There Are Exceptions to Every Rule:
Shake Crème Liqueurs

When you see the word *crème* on a bottle of liqueur it doesn't mean dairy, it means sugar. A bottle of liquor is normally about 40% alcohol (80 proof) and 60% water. A liqueur is at least 2.5% sugar by weight (most of them have much more), but a crème liqueur is over 40% sugar. Crème liqueurs are much more like alcoholic syrups. Thus, they can be poured over pancakes or, more to the point, they must be shaken when making cocktails.

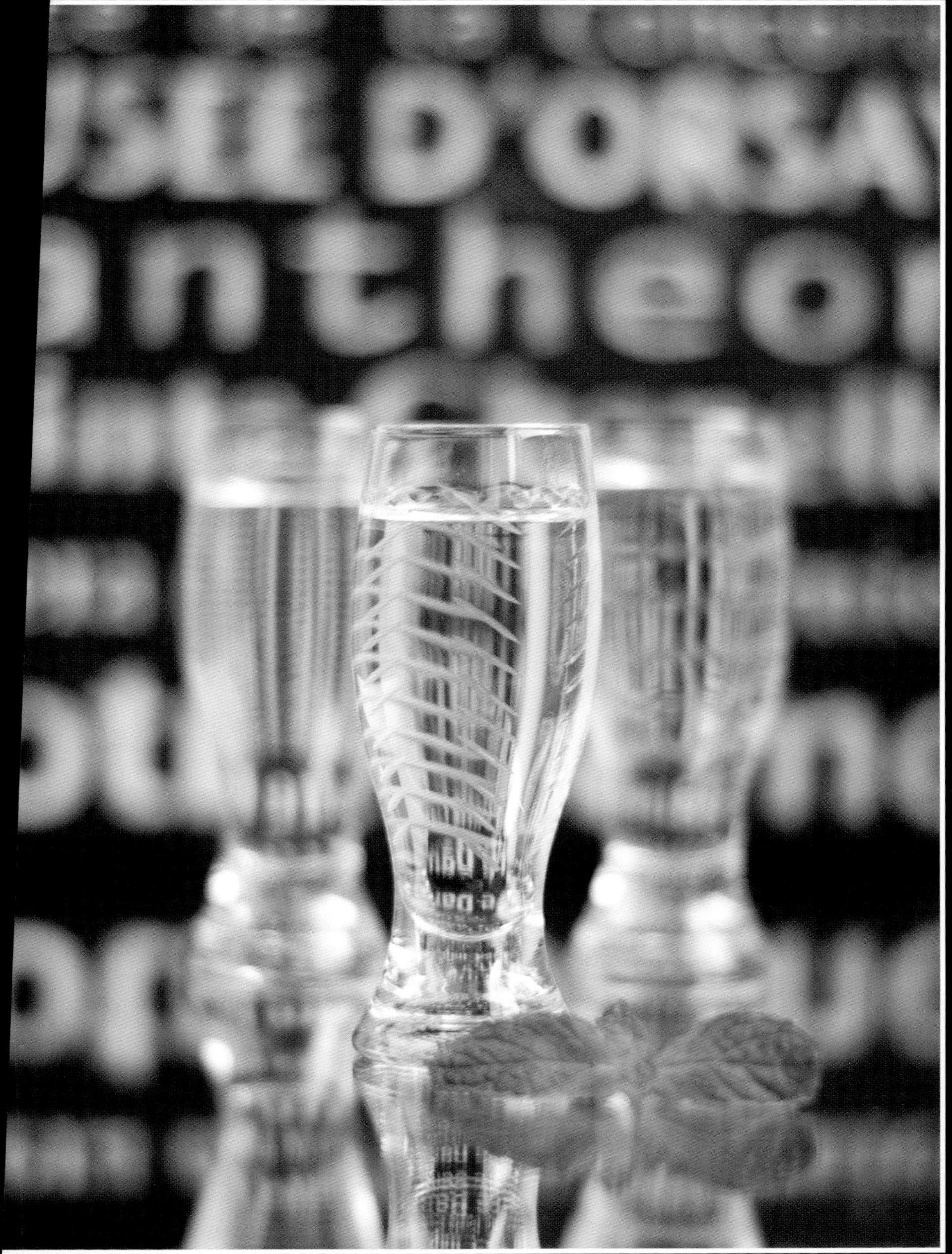

Between the Sheets

In the world of drinking there is plenty of room for bawdy drink names. This is one of an all-time favorite "you're going to know you had a drink" cocktails. Even when brought down to tiny shot-sized proportions, this little devil will bring out your dark side. This shot is dangerous because the balance is so perfect you won't realize how strong it really is. The Between the Sheets is best served to those unafraid of dancing on tabletops.

MAKES

.5 ounce light rum

.5 ounce cognac

.5 ounce Cointreau

.25 ounce fresh lemon juice

1. Shake and strain into a shot glass.

Splitting Up the Base Spirit:
How to Put the "B" in Subtle

The Between the Sheets shot uses equal parts of three different 80 proof liquors. This allows you to get little highlights from each spirit as they all comingle into a deliciously wicked shot. Rum lightens up the vanilla edge of the cognac and both liquors blend perfectly with the orange of the triple sec.

Brett Ashley

If you get stood up at a bar, you might as well get drunk. Or less belligerently, many classic cocktails have enjoyed fifteen minutes of fame at some point and that is what this cocktail is about. Jake Barnes, one of literature's great sad bastards, sat at the bar and got stood up by the Lady Brett Ashley while drinking a Jack Rose cocktail. This happened in The Sun Also Rises *by Ernest Hemingway; your high school reading list has come back to haunt you. The Jack Rose has had an amazing renaissance in drinking culture for two reasons—neither of which have to do with Jake. The first is that it is delicious, and the second is that it is cheap.*

MAKES

1 ounce applejack

.5 ounce Grenadine

.25 ounce lemon juice

1. Shake and strain into a shot glass.

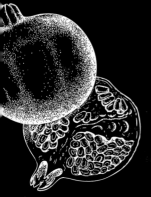

Grenadine:
If You Don't Know What It Is, You've Never Had It

Grenadine is neither red sugar syrup nor the stuff from the cherry jar. Grenadine is a pomegranate syrup. And while it is sometimes hard to find the real stuff, it is very easy to make some yourself. Grab a bottle of pomegranate juice, pour it into a pan, and throw it on the stove. Let it boil for a minute and then stir in and dissolve an equal part of sugar. You can fancy it up from here, but that is the most basic way to get the job done.

Pink Dale

Dale Degroff will be the first to tell you that he didn't invent the Cosmopolitan. On his behalf, the Cosmopolitan can be a great drink when made properly, but when it is half-assed there could not be a more pedestrian cocktail. The Pink Dale is a tribute to Dale Degroff's version of the Cosmopolitan, which—accept it or not—is one of the most influential drinks ever.

MAKES

.5 ounce citrus vodka

.5 ounce triple sec

.25 ounce cranberry juice

1 lime wedge

1 orange zest

1. Shake the first four ingredients and strain into a shot glass.

2. Spritz the top of the cocktail with a flamed orange zest.

The Flamed Orange Zest:
A Way to Show Off Your Bartending Skills

Did you know that citrus oil is flammable? If you delicately cut a little peel off of an orange (or any citrus) and squeeze it peel-side toward a flame, you'll get a little burst of flame. If you have an ant farm at home, doing a few dozen of these in a row would be a little Fourth of July for those guys. But when you do it atop a cocktail you get a lightly bittersweet edge and aroma on a cocktail.

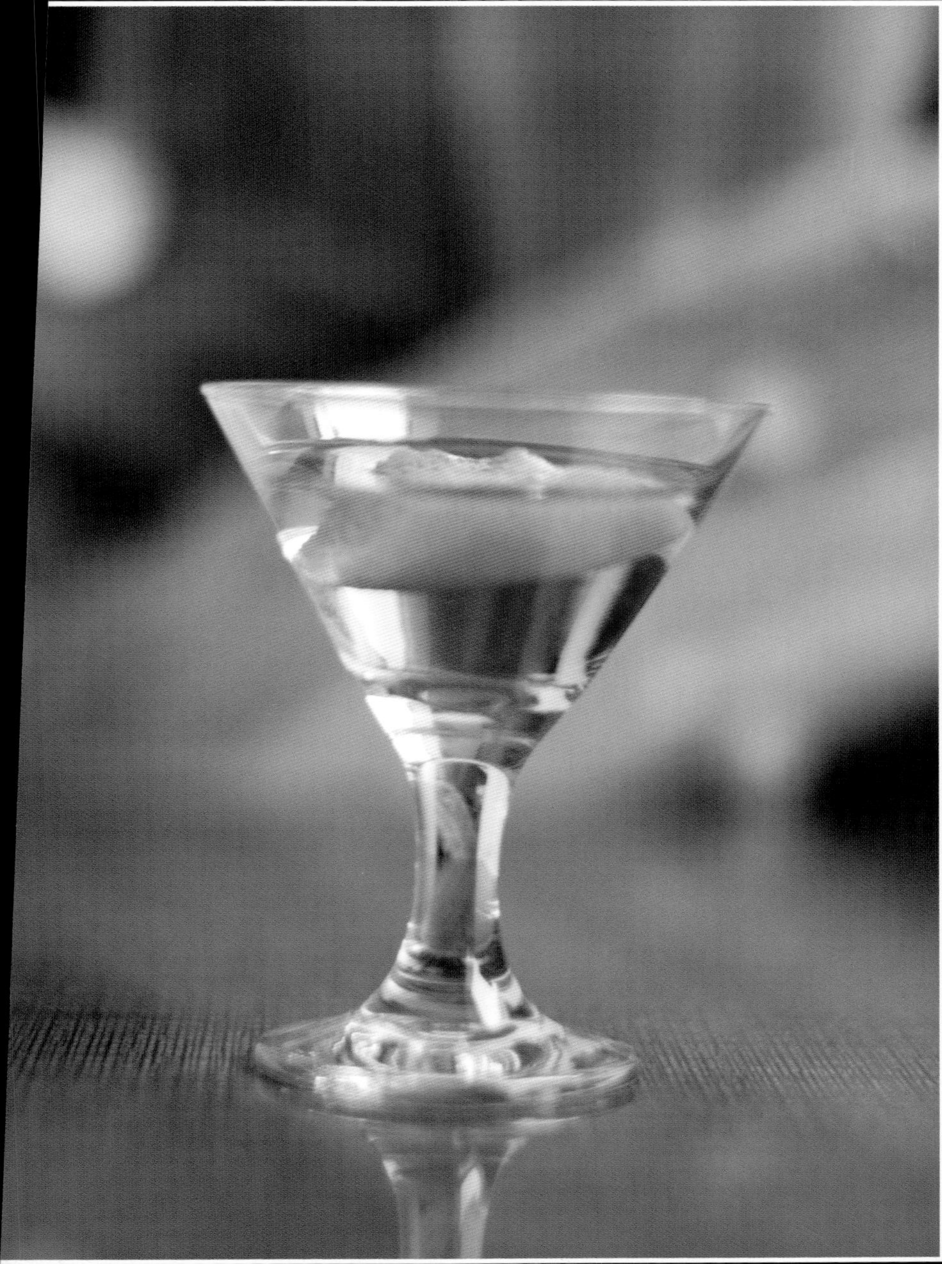

Blue Briar

There once was a man from New Zealand, a land where supposedly there are still dragons and everyone walks on their hands. This man was named Jacob Briars, and his absurdity was only exceeded by his skill to wear a rubber horse-head mask. Jacob is by all accounts a silly man. He also almost single-handedly saved a generation of bartenders from being too serious. The Blue Briar is a play on an old-fashioned cocktail called the Corpse Reviver #2. It's all a tribute to his defense of blue curaçao. In the world of alcohol, even in the world of single malt Scotch, artificial coloring is quite common.

MAKES

1 ounce Lillet Blanc

.5 ounce London dry gin

.5 ounce Cointreau

1 dash blue curaçao

1 dash absinthe

1. Shake and strain into a shot glass.

What Is Blue Curaçao?

Blue curaçao is a sweet (and should be aromatic) liqueur flavored with the dried peel of the laraha citrus fruit, which is a little runty citrus similar to an orange. When this orange–ish spirit comes off the still it is, like every freshly distilled spirit, crystal clear. Over curaçao's 400–year production history, every color in the rainbow has been added to it.

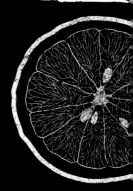

Wallaby Kick

Before James Bond drank vodka martinis he drank Vespers. Before Ian Fleming ever penned a Bond novel there was a commonly known cocktail consisting of three parts vodka to one part dry vermouth called a Kangaroo Kicker. And on top of that, the instructions for this original recipe states, "Shaken not stirred." The Wallaby Kick is a tribute to the vodka martini, but we'll be shaking up mostly dry vermouth for this very mature secret agent shot. If you think this sounds like too intense of a shot, read on about vermouth.

MAKES

1 ounce dry vermouth

.5 ounce vodka

1 green olive, chilled

1. Shake the first two ingredients and strain into a shot glass.
2. Chase with a cold green olive.

Vermouth: *It's Not Poison*

Did you know that vermouth is an aromatized wine? That is to say, it's a wine infused with herbs and spices and then fortified with brandy. The most important part of that definition is the fact that vermouth is a wine: Vermouth lives and dies like a wine. If you opened a bottle that has been sitting at home for a year, then congratulations—you now have made "small batch artisan vinegar." Always keep vermouth in the fridge.

Pequeña Daisy

Julio Bermejo and his wife, Elmy, are two of the most important people in the tequila world, but it's likely that you've never heard of them. They oversee, run, live, and breathe one of the best (if not the best) tequila collections in the world at San Francisco's legendary Tommy's. Julio is also most responsible for the trend of using agave nectar to sweeten a Margarita. Tequila has fought a long battle to not be blended on ice or shot like medicine. It is almost a shame to offer a tiny Margarita as a shot. However, the Pequeña Daisy takes a Margarita back to its simplest and more pure form, and that is a cause for celebration.

MAKES

1 ounce reposado tequila

.25 ounce agave nectar

.25 ounce lime juice

1. Shake and strain into a shot glass (optional: a salt-rimmed cocktail glass).

When Was the Margarita Invented?

Many people claim to have invented some sort of Margarita in the 1940s. If it seems odd to you that someone would claim to have invented something so simple, well, you are right. In 1882, a book called *The Flowing Bowl* first published a cocktail concept called a "Daisy." The Daisy cocktail template is a spirit with lime and some sort of liqueur sweetener, usually an orange. To put the last piece of the puzzle in place: *Margarita* means *Daisy* in Spanish.

Frisco Kid

There is no easier way to get a person from San Francisco angry than by calling the city San Fran or Frisco. The Frisco Kid is an abbreviated and improved Frisco cocktail. The combination of herbal Benedictine and sweet and spicy rye makes a shot for those who want a shot to get through the dark days of the San Francisco August. The orange bitters add high notes and aroma that make this shot perfect for a "thick sweater and umbrella" kind of day.

MAKES

.75 ounce rye whiskey

.75 ounce Benedictine

2 dashes orange bitters

1. Stir and strain into a shot glass.

Benedictine: *It Wasn't Invented in the 1970s*

At over 500 years old, Benedictine is the world's oldest liqueur brand. Benedictine is a cognac-based herbal liqueur that is said to be a secret recipe. While that's a fine story for the back of a cereal box, the modern Food and Drug administration doesn't allow secret recipes. A fun exercise for those with too much space in their refrigerator is doing online research for homemade vermouth, bitters, and liqueurs. Many classic secret formulas are "cracked" for your home experiments, but don't tell your significant other you got the idea from this book.

Double Entendre

Hanky panky used to mean "cool." It isn't certain how exactly it came to mean "having sexy times," but Ada Coleman defined the Hanky Panky Cocktail in 1925. The original cocktail is quite complex and mature, which is also code for "most people hate it." You should give this smoothed out version a try for its touch of minty freshness with an herbal finish. The original Hanky Panky used London dry gin. For this version, we'll be switching it to genever to add more body to the shot. Genever is a full-flavored but less herbal ancestor of gin.

MAKES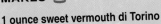

1 ounce sweet vermouth di Torino

.5 ounce genever

1 dash Fernet Branca

1 orange zest

1. Stir first three ingredients and strain into a shot glass.

2. Spritz with an orange zest.

Phrase of the Day:

"I'm Here to See a Man about a Horse"

The phrase today means, "I'm going to the bathroom." But "I'm here to see a man about a horse" originally meant that one was going to get a drink. Specifically, during prohibition it meant, "Let me into this speakeasy; I want a drink." And those speakeasies were referred to as "blind pigs" or "blind tigers."

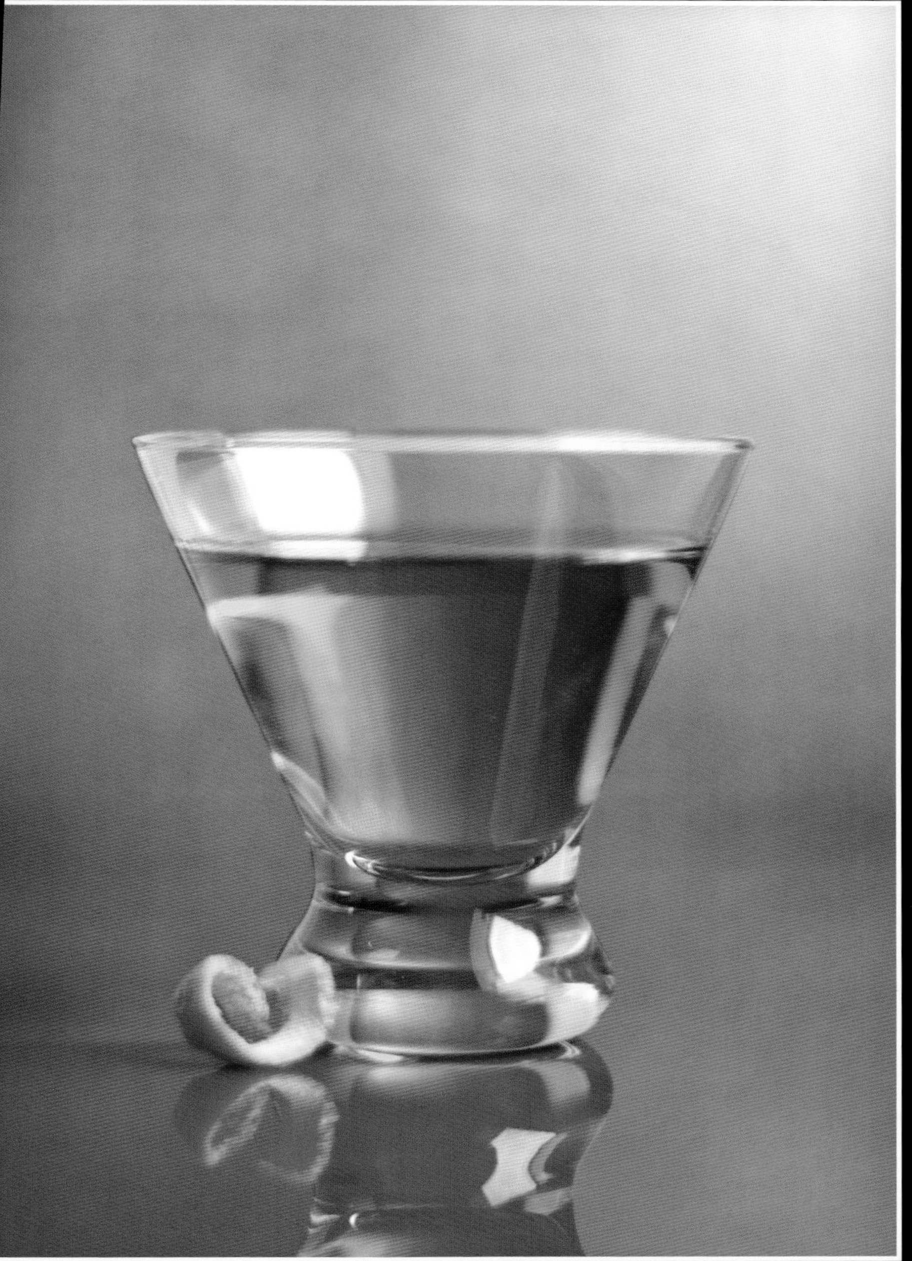

Pendennis Treehouse

A long time ago in a place called the United States, we drank in private clubs and dining halls. True, this was an exclusionary way for high society to maintain connections, but it was also the best way to skirt liquor laws. The Pendennis Club in Louisville, Kentucky, is one of the classiest private clubs still around. Their eponymous cocktail is a perfect balance on the palate. The Pendennis Treehouse is like the children's version of that cocktail.

MAKES

1 ounce gin

.25 ounce lime cordial

1 tablespoon apricot or
   peach preserves

2 dashes Peychaud's bitters

1. Shake very hard and strain into a shot glass.

In the Club

Stork, Pegu, Clover, Jockey: What do all of these drinks have in common? They are all eponymous cocktails of their respective clubs. Though they are mostly lost to obscurity and prohibitive ingredients, they are still known by the bartenders who are very, very old. Let them also be an inspiration to create a house cocktail and force it upon every guest that comes into your home.

Orgeat Shot

This cocktail is inspired by the classic: The Barbancourt Rum Cup. Orgeat is the secret ingredient of countless tiki drinks. It is just as essential as the crushed ice itself. But it often gets overlooked or substituted for some other almond liqueur (or worse: just some syrupy goo). But the Orgeat Shot can't go it alone, it needs backup from Jamaican rum, the funkiest rum of all. These two paired together create the perfect balance and mystery flavor from any tiki drink. But to remove a bit of mystery, you can use this shot as the basis for any drink with an umbrella.

MAKES

1 ounce Jamaican rum

.5 ounce orgeat syrup

.25 ounce lime juice

1. Shake and strain into a shot glass. Garnish with a paper umbrella.

What Is Orgeat?

Orgeat is syrup made from almonds and orange flower water, and when you're lucky, it's an almond liqueur. It is rare in the United States, but it is making a comeback in craft cocktail bars and coffee stands. Yes, this elusive syrup is more likely to be poured by a barista than a tiki bartender. The good news is that it's as easy to make as adding sugar and orange flower water to almond milk. By no means the best, but a quick and dirty way to make orgeat is to warm up 18 ounces of almond milk and dissolve in an equal part of sugar. Let the mixture cool and then add 1 ounce orange flower water. Most grocery stores carry orange flower water next to the soda pop. Bottle it up and it will stay good in the fridge for a month.

Spicy Shirley

The Spicy Shirley makes that Shirley Temple into a shot that you cannot tame. The addition of cinnamon syrup and vodka takes a cute child star and turns her into a fiery little redhead. On the flipside of the Spicy Shirley, let's talk about cinnamon in this drink. Cinnamon has been part of the booze world for a long time and every incarnation of it boasts (falsely) furious monikers. Without brand bashing, let's consider what the word "cinnamon" brings to mind. A rough and tough shooter or perhaps the name of a little girl's puppy dog? The Spicy Shirley is also here to remind you that these cinnamon shots, well, they ain't so tough.

MAKES

1 ounce vodka

.5 ounce cinnamon syrup

1. Shake and strain into a shot glass.

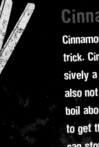

Cinnamon Syrup

Cinnamon syrup is just as easy to make as it sounds, but there is one little trick. Cinnamon is almost the perfect definition of something that is exclusively a smell, meaning that it has almost no flavor other than "bitter." It is also not very water-soluble. When making cinnamon syrup, you will have to boil about 4 whole cinnamon sticks for about 20 minutes in a pint of water to get the flavor out of them. Then mix in equal parts sugar by volume. You can store your syrup in the fridge for up to a month.

Part 2

BANGERS & SLAMMERS

t's not that the Harvey Wallbanger was ever the best that mixology had to offer, but it certainly is the most fun drink to order. Wallbanger. Say it: *Wallbanger*. Awesome. The intense silliness of Galliano liqueur's anise and vanilla flavor is what makes the Harvey Wallbanger such a great drink. The same can be said of the foolishness behind the Tequila Slammer. If that youthful folly and gaiety could have a baby, it would be the mix of lemon-lime soda and tequila slammed down on the bar. It would be a Tequila Slammer. While the merits of the Tequila Slammer and the Harvey Wallbanger should always be in question, the simplicity and jollity of the two should never be questioned. This chapter of Bangers & Slammers honor these simple, silly drinks from the college years, and they'll also all feature effervescence or silly anise liqueurs. Remember, to add Galliano just say, "Make mine a banger!"

French 70 Slammer

A lot of people think the French 75 should be a cognac pastry, but in actuality it's a cocktail that was invented in the United States, which is why it uses gin. The original French 75 is indeed a cocktail named for giant cannons mounted on train cars, but the French 70 Slammer is the Saturday night special version of that cocktail. To get the full bang out of this cocktail you'll need to chill the gin in advance and make the champagne ice cold before pouring the two together in each shot glass. When you add the simple syrup, just pour a touch at the bottom of each glass.

MAKES

.5 ounce gin

.5 ounce simple syrup

top with champagne

1. Pour the first two ingredients into a shot glass, top with champagne, and slam.

Champagne Is Only Champagne

Go ahead and pick a sparkling wine like prosecco if you're just planning to mix it with orange juice at a baby shower. If you're making quality cocktails, only use the real thing. There are dozens of grower champagnes on the market for half the price of larger houses' bottlings, so try something new.

Invisible Rabbit

The parable of the elephant in the room is quite useful, but perhaps a better known story is that of Harvey, the six-foot-three-and-one-half-inch-tall invisible rabbit. Perhaps the moral of the story from the film Harvey is to accept people's eccentricities. And perhaps as James Stewart did in the film, ordering one martini for yourself and one martini for your invisible friend is completely acceptable. Even more so, it makes the bartender like you.

MAKES

.75 ounce gin

.75 ounce dry vermouth

Lemon-lime soda

1. Pour the first two ingredients into a shot glass, top with lemon-lime soda, and slam.

How Do You Chill a Slammer?

Room temperature gin and vermouth are fine for ex-members of the British OSS to drink while they reminisce about the Cold War, but normal folks might want that gin to be chilled a bit. If you plan to make an Invisible Rabbit, you will need to chill the ingredients, and in the case of gin, it should just be kept in the freezer, only to be removed to get "ginned up."

Whiskey Buck Hunter

There's usually a cooler way to order any drink at the bar. If you'd like vodka and orange juice, tell the bartender you want a Screwdriver, and if gin and grapefruit juice is your thing, call it a Salty Dog. You can add ginger ale to any drink by calling it a Buck. A little shot of whiskey and ginger really wakes you up when you slam it down quickly. It is also the perfect drink to throw back when you're in a dive bar playing Buckhunter. Remember two things: Blaze orange saves lives and you lose points for shooting cows.

MAKES

1 ounce bourbon

2 dashes Angostura bitters

1 squeeze of a lime

.25 ounce ginger beer

1. Pour first three ingredients into a glass, top with ginger beer, and slam.

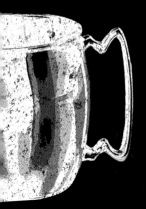

Moscow Mule Mug: *Why a Copper Mug?*

The Moscow Mule is back on the rise. Everyone loves it. It's easy to make and easier to drink. The Moscow Mule was invented in Los Angeles in 1941 by the owner of Cock & Bull ginger beer and a marketing guy from Smirnoff. The simple combination of vodka and ginger beer was something so perfectly pleasing and simple that only nonbartenders could come up with it. However it was the Dutch copper mugs that made the drink stick. Sure, copper conducts cold better than glass, but it was really about creating a ritual for drinking—a ritual that bartenders now use to overcharge for a vodka and ginger beer. Whiskey and ginger show up together in several different cocktail incarnations like the Presbyterian or the Horse's Neck.

Seel-Banger

Al Capone loved the Seelbach Hotel in Louisville, Kentucky. He loved it so much that he had secret passages there to evade law enforcement that might be interested in taking down the bootlegger. He could always be found drinking the house cocktail at the Seelbach, a combination of bitters, bourbon, and triple sec. As a cocktail, this dry drink is not for many, but it makes a really fun slammer.

MAKES

.5 ounce triple sec

.25 ounce bourbon

2 dashes Peychaud's bitters

2 dashes Angostura bitters

.25 ounce champagne

1. Stir and strain the first four ingredients into a shot glass.
2. Top with champagne and slam.

Angostura & Peychaud's:
A Cocktail Duo That Creates Balance

As mentioned earlier, Peychaud's adds dryness to a cocktail and Angostura adds a kind of baking spice sweetness. Peychaud's is your dry, acid-witted friend and Angostura is your aunt who is obsessed with Christmas. These great bitters do very different things in cocktails, so make sure to balance these two for the right combination.

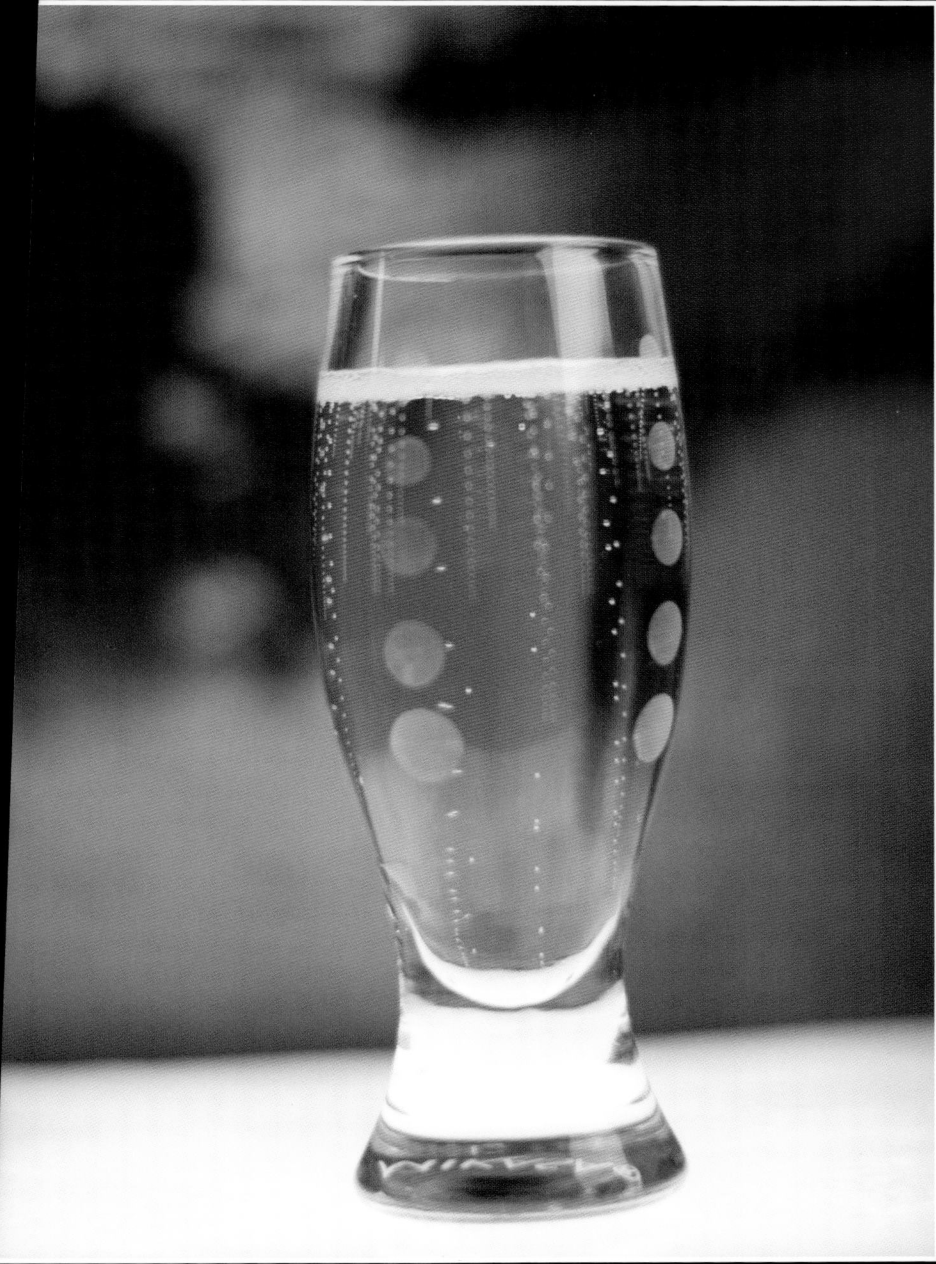

Tweedy Slammer

Not that anybody cares, but blended Scotch is what most of the world wants when they ask for a whiskey. This is okay, and even better for mixing cocktails. In Spain one of the most preferred ways to drink whiskey is blended Scotch and ginger ale. It really is an amazing combination of Scotch's light smoke and a little bit of ginger's fire. I envision the Tweedy Slammer as an alternate reality for the Tequila Slammer. In a different timeline, if the Tequila Slammer had been invented at an Edinburgh University pub in 1905, it would be the Tweedy Slammer we'd all know from college.

MAKES

1 ounce blended Scotch

.25 ounce lime juice

2 ounces ginger beer

1. Pour ingredients into a shot glass and slam.

Ginger Ale vs. Ginger Beer:
What Is the Difference?

To put it in a modern context but not necessarily a historical one, think of them like this. Ginger beer is brewed or cooked with ginger, lemon, and sugar; some brands have alcohol as a result. Ginger beer has a big spicy flavor. While ginger ale has a similar flavor, it is a soda product and is much lighter and sweeter.

Cider Press

An actual cider press is a giant wooden bucket from colonial America used to press apples into submission. It does look as if it is a terrible contraption that is used to torture people. Perhaps in olden days, they used to throw a witch into the ol' cider press every now and then. But the Cider Press for you will instead tap into the American tradition of apple cider, bourbon, and mild irresponsibility toward heavy inebriation.

MAKES

1 ounce bourbon

.5 ounce apple cider

1 ounce lemon-lime soda

1. Pour ingredients into a shot glass and slam.

As American as Apple Brandy

Europeans brought apples to America for what would seem to be drinking purposes more than anything else. We made hard cider (*hard* means with booze) and awful apple brandy. We would later begin to stretch out our apple brandy with the addition of whiskey—thus applejack was refined into something more palatable.

This cocktail uses bourbon instead of apple brandy to add new flavors. Bourbon's rich, sweet-and-spicy flavors support the apple cider instead of being lost in it. Apple brandy and apple juice with apple bitters doesn't make for an interesting cocktail; it would just taste like a variety of apples instead of having its own unique flavor. Bourbon brings complexity to this shot.

Ricky's Jab

Another great and long-lost cocktail term is quite simply the Ricky. What does Ricky mean? Simple: lime soda booze. All too often I hear a bartender assailed with this type of request: "I'll have a vodka soda with three limes; maybe muddle limes in the bottom of the glass." It seems that people forget that with our modern technology (remember the Internet?) we also now have the ability to squeeze limes to extract their juice into a glass using a contraption called a juicer. We need not muddle a bunch of garbage into the bottom of a glass anymore. And quite simply put, it's very easy to say, "Vodka Ricky." You can even throw a "please" on that if you like.

MAKES

1 ounce vodka

.5 ounce lime cordial

1 ounce soda

 Pour ingredients into a shot glass and slam.

Lime Cordial: *You Should Make Your Own*

Making lime cordial is about as easy as mixing sugar and water with three other ingredients, but it's still not very difficult. You can play around with the ingredients to get your own specific recipe, but every recipe calls for a simple syrup. You then add about one-third lime juice to that mix, put in just a whisper of citric acid, and voilà—you have a lime cordial! Don't see citric acid on the shelf next to the baking soda? Wine-making supply stores usually carry it. Homemade lime cordial won't last forever like the stuff you buy at the grocery store but it will taste much better.

Showgirl

The Showgirl shot is not named for the best worst movie ever; it's a play on what we used to call Showgirl's Milk. Showgirl's Milk combines bitters, a sugar cube, and champagne in the only champagne cocktail for these starlets. And even if you're not on your feet all day kicking in a chorus line while being leered at, you can take great respite in a cocktail like this.

MAKES

1 Angostura-soaked sugar cube

3 ounces champagne

1. Place the Angostura-soaked sugar cube into a shot glass.
2. Add champagne.
3. Allow a couple seconds for sugar and champagne to react and then slam.

How to Transform a $7 Bottle of Sparkling Wine into an Amazing Toast

Showgirl is a great shot to serve en masse since preparation is simple. To start making this shot, pour as many shots of sparkling wine as you'd like; a standard 750ml bottle makes twenty-four shots. Then hold a sugar cube atop of a bottle of Angostura bitters with one finger and turn the bottle upside down. This will soak the sugar cube with bitters. Make one intoxicating sugar cube for each shot and drop them in just before serving. Warn people about the sugar cube to prevent choking hazards.

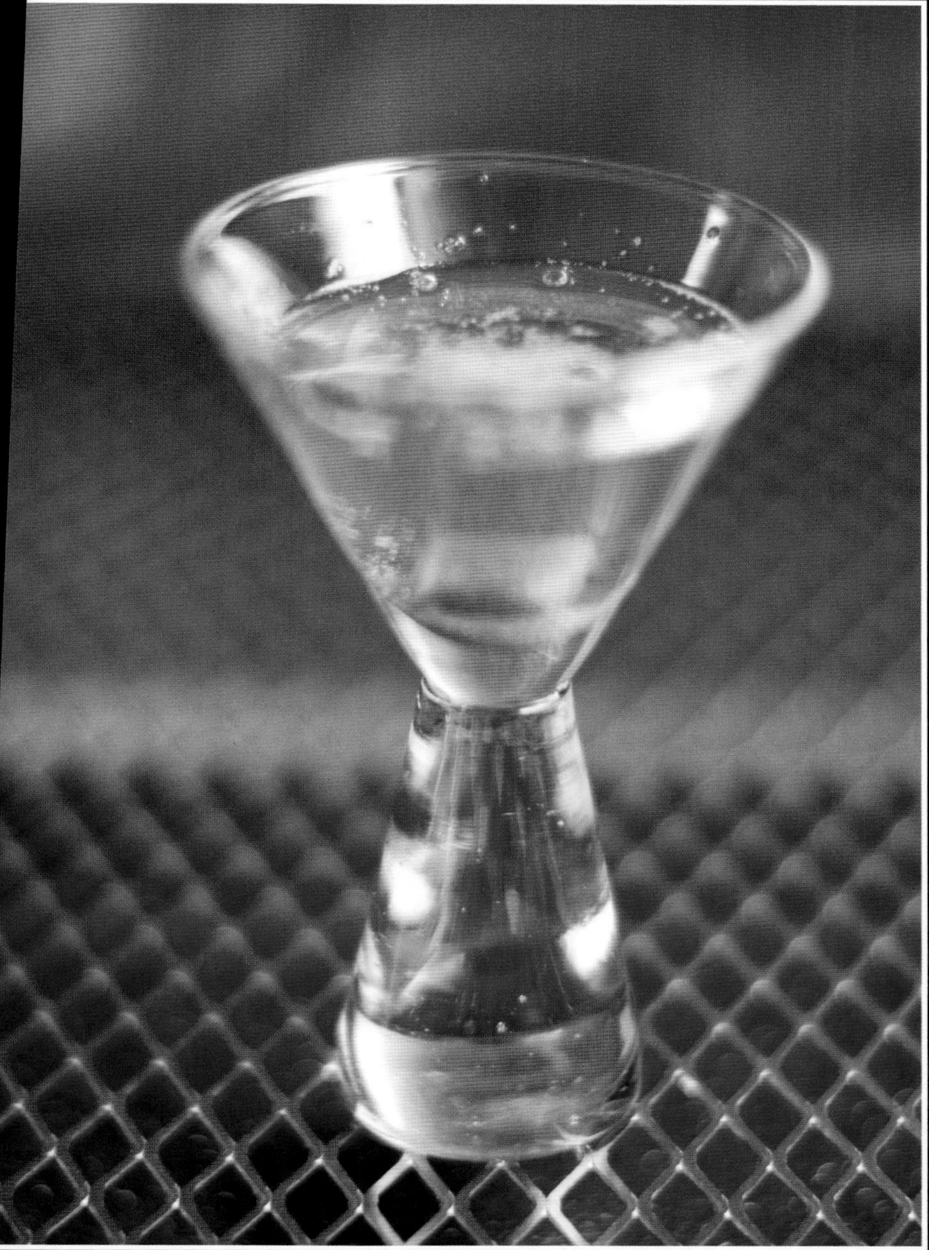

Diablita

The Diablo cocktail should be the "other" tequila cocktail that everyone knows. It was invented by Trader Vic for his chain of Mexican restaurants in the 1950s. The original cocktail is made with tequila, ginger beer, lime juice, and crème de cassis. For our shooter version, we are going to make it a slammer. This is one of the few times you should be shooting tequila.

MAKES

1 ounce reposado tequila

.25 ounce crème de cassis

.25 ounce lime juice

2 ounces ginger beer

1. Pour ingredients into a shot glass and slam.

Cassis:
Nobody Really Knows What That Is, But You Should

Cassis shows up in lots of cocktails and people often substitute it with Chambord. Because of Chambord's deliciousness, nobody really complains, but Chambord is a black raspberry liqueur and cassis is a black currant liqueur. It may not seem like a huge difference, but it is like asking for apples and being given pears.

The Moscow Mule Made Mexican

The Diablo is basically a Moscow Mule with tequila and a dash of cassis instead of vodka. This was Trader Vic's way of working smarter, not harder. Keep that in mind when creating your own new drinks.

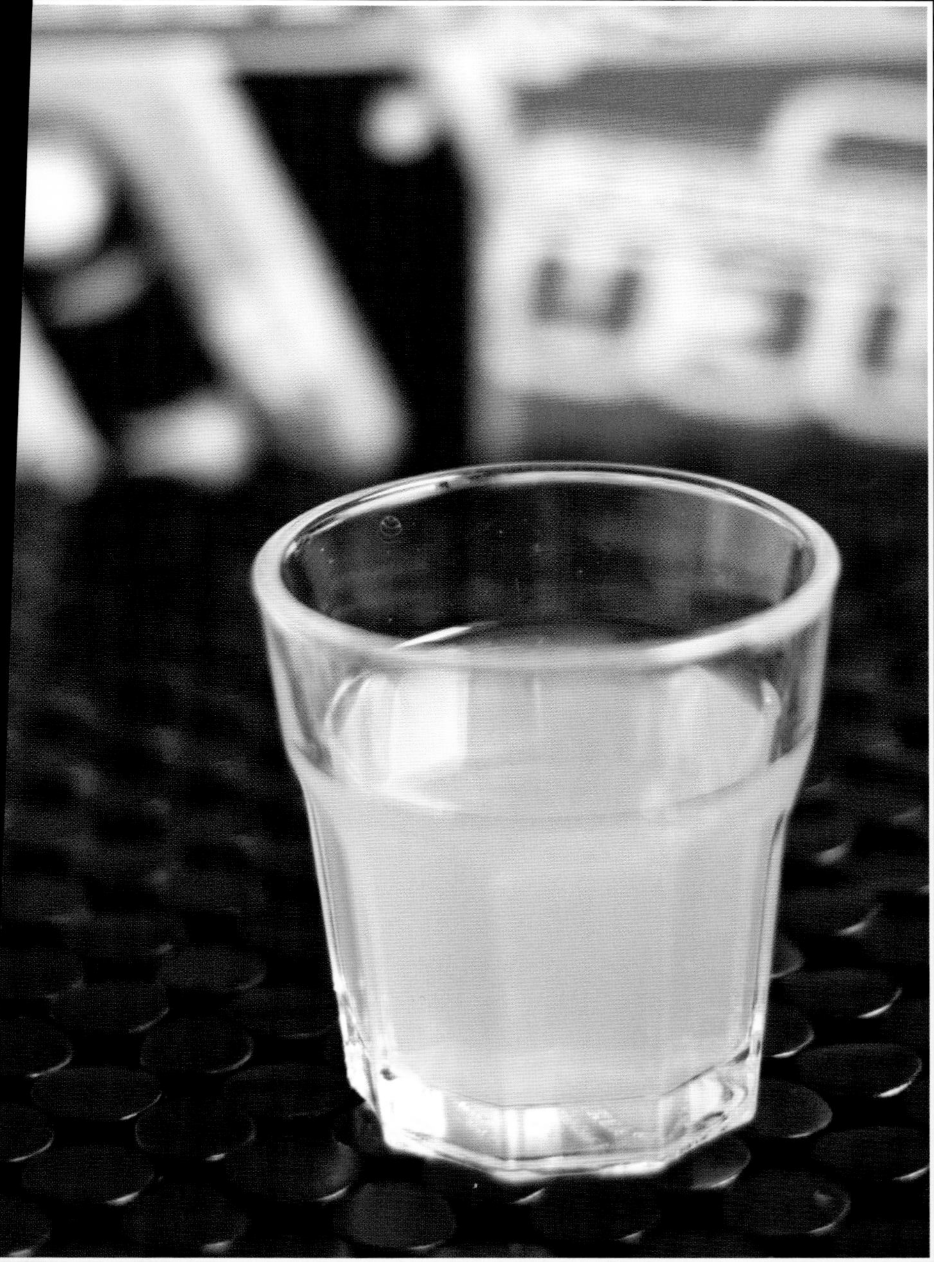

Wallbanger

The Harvey Wallbanger takes Galliano, an unwieldy misunderstood bottle, and makes it into an ingredient that is as perfect as a haiku. People will tell you that a surfer named Harvey had too many of these at a party and banged into the wall repeatedly on the way out the door. While we all know this as a viable story, it is not the truth. The Harvey Wallbanger is actually one of the many creations of Donato "Duke" Antone. It was invented in 1952, but became the iconic drink of the 1970s.

MAKES

1 ounce vodka

1 ounce orange juice

.5 ounce Galliano

1. Shake and strain ingredients into a shot glass.

Fun Facts about Galliano

The trademark seventeen-inch bottle is patterned after a Roman column, and it works very well as a paper towel roll holder. Many drinks with Galliano have the word *wall* in their name, but adding Galliano really makes it quite the banger! Currently, the sweet 60 proof liqueur is reformulating to a drier 84.6 proof alcohol, so you can learn all new ways to enjoy it.

Uyeda's Crystal

The Japanese bartender Kazuo Uyeda was well known for creating a drink style called corals. Corals are salt-rimmed glasses that use an aromatic liqueur to adhere the salt to the glass. Uyeda had a cocktail called the Crystal Coral, which is a dry interpretation of a Paloma with a touch of blue curaçao. Uyeda's Crystal is a miniaturized version of that coral cocktail.

MAKES

.25 ounce blue curaçao

1 pinch salt

1 ounce tequila

1 ounce grapefruit juice

1. Dip the top of the shot glass into a dish of blue curaçao and then into salt.

2. Pour remaining ingredients into shot glass and slam.

It's All Mixing Tequila (Almost)

You can mix with any tequila that you can afford, but in general, mix with reposados and bigger-flavored tequilas. Remember, tequila comes from a delicate flower, so un-aged tequila and lighter tequila will be lost in most mixed drinks.

Punching Bag

It's not necessarily bad to be a punching bag. While some people associate punching bags with boxing or a release of anger, it's best to associate it with this deliciously fresh take on a shot. The Punching Bag pairs seemingly different ingredients together to create a classic flavor. Berries are a natural sparring partner to the herbal anise flavors in aquavit. To enjoy this cocktail to its fullest potential, try using fresh raspberries.

MAKES

1 ounce aquavit

.5 ounce simple syrup

4 whole raspberries

1. Shake very hard and strain into a shot glass.

Why Use Raspberries Instead of Raspberry Syrup?

Raspberry syrup is great for sodas and pancakes, or for creating fake crime scenes. While it tastes great, it doesn't smell like much, so using fresh raspberries lets you enjoy the fresh aroma of the season.

Savatuer

Savate is a French form of kickboxing that uses feet and occasionally weapons. A savatuer is a person who practices this graceful yet intense sport, and although this bit of lexicon is rarely of use, it is the perfect inspiration for this kickpuncher shot.

MAKES

1 ounce yellow Chartreuse

.25 ounce brandy

.25 ounce lemon juice

2 dashes grapefruit bitters

1. Shake and strain into a shot glass.

Yellow Chartreuse Is Not Like Green

Green Chartreuse is the better-known bottling in the Chartreuse family. It is 110 proof and therefore viciously intense. Yellow Chartreuse is considered its sweeter, gentler, and floral brother. At 80 proof, it pairs much better with fruit tea and other herbal flavors.

Prizefighter

Ask 100 people what they got out of the film Rocky and some of them will tell you that Sylvester Stallone is an amazing actor while others will tell you that drinking eggs makes you strong. The Prizefighter is a cocktail with a victorious name to make people feel safe about drinking a whole egg. It may not make you a better boxer, but any bar patron or experienced bartender can tell you it makes you a better fighter.

MAKES

1 ounce rum

.5 ounce simple syrup

1 whole egg

2 dashes hot sauce

1. Shake and fine strain into a shot glass.

Is It Safe to Drink a Raw Egg?

Scientifically speaking, most doctors would advise against it for children, the elderly, and people with immunodeficiency problems. But the rest of you people have no excuse. If you drink homemade eggnog, you are drinking raw eggs already. It's also safe to say that you have probably seen all too many people dig down deep into a pocket or purse to find one last dusty breath mint, and that's grosser than drinking the ova of any animal.

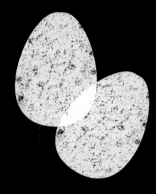

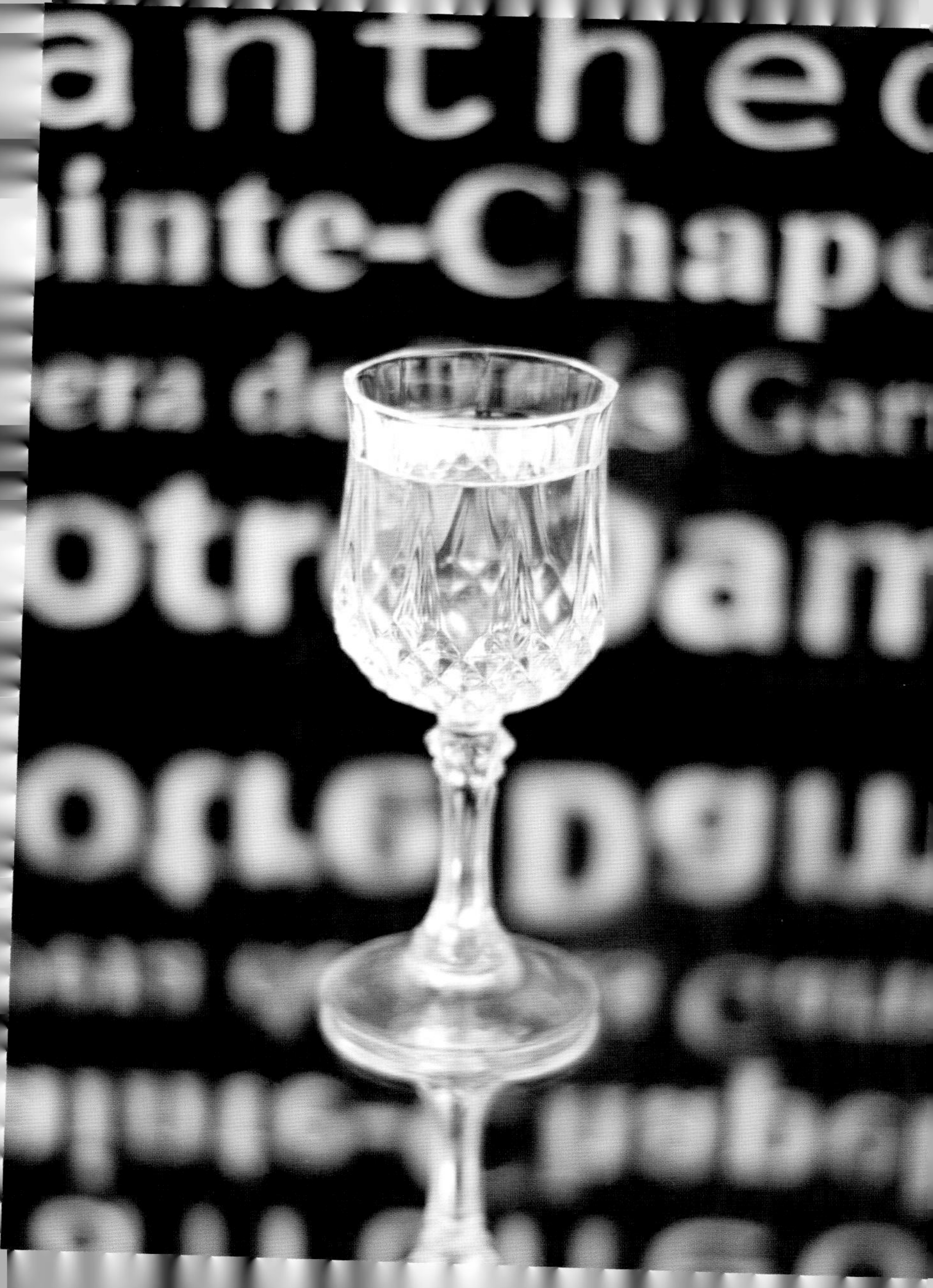

Curtains for Polonius

Considering the number of volumes that the man wrote and his love for drinking, it is a shame that more cocktails aren't named for Shakespeare. This one comes straight from Hamlet, a play dense enough to inspire thousands of murderous, revenge-soaked shots. Like the dagger that did Polonius in, this is a crisp, sharp shot—and definitely a good one to take before you start monologues.

MAKES

1 ounce akavit

.5 ounce vodka

.25 ounce simple syrup

1. Shake and fine strain into a shot glass.

It's All About Akavit

Akavit is basically the herbal vodka of Northern Europe, and that is how it is made. Vodka is re-distilled with herbs and spices, most notably dill and caraway. But unlike most any other spirit, akavit needs an extra step to earn its name that has nothing to do with production rules or appellation. It must be taken out to sea for a voyage. Some just go out and back while others literally go around the world.

Part 3

FARMERS' MARKET

n the winter it is our collective job as citizens of earth to try to drink Scotland dry of single malts. But n the spring, summer, and fall, all of the goodness the world has to offer is at the farmers' market. The best thing to do with seasonal produce is to drink t. Apples are great but apple cider is better. Fresh raspberries are beautiful but vodka makes them shine. Go to the liquor store every Saturday and then back to the farmers' market every Sunday. Be ready with two shopping lists: drinking and eating. This is certainly the secret to happiness.

The best part about using fresh fruit is that you won't need a muddler. If the fruit is ripe, ice will usu-ally do all of the muddling for you. However, don't run to the market at the first sign of fresh produce—that first round of fruit and vegetables is for suckers since it is harvested way too early. Before you get to cooking up the goodies from a trip to the farmers' market, make sure you sample the flavors by pairing your produce with the alcohol in these shots.

Spiced Peach

If a peach is truly ripe, only the most delicate hands of a brain surgeon can touch it without bruising it. Luckily for everyone else, bruised peaches are a gift for drinking. Peaches pair well with most herbs, but we'll use the simple spice of thyme for this recipe. If you really want to make this drink in an advanced way, split a peach in half and grill it before throwing it into the shaker.

MAKES

1 ounce Drambuie

1 ounce vodka

.5 ounce lemon juice

1 peach half

4 sprigs of thyme

1. Shake hard and fine strain into a shot glass.

2. Makes two drinks.

Drambuie: *Not a* Dungeons & Dragons *Character*

Drambuie is a Scotch liqueur that is flavored with heather, saffron, and clove before it is sweetened with honey. Most know it as a dusty bottle in Dad's liquor cabinet, but it is so much more. There is an epic and mythical past behind the liqueur. Sure, it may not involve elves, but there are plenty of princes and kings in its tale. The story of Drambuie's origin is dubious, but it takes place a couple hundred years ago in a part of Scotland that belongs in *The Lord of the Rings*.

Menthe Nymph

Before the Mojito, it seemed like mint was just for toothpaste. To the ancient Greeks, however, the nymph Menthe was the foxy minx who stole the heart of Hades. When his wife found out, she tried to kill Menthe, but Hades transformed Menthe into a shrub to always keep her growing and free. This shot's name is derived from the minty nymph's tie-in with one of Greece's most feared spirits: ouzo. The Greeks traditionally, medicinally, and recreationally take shots of this anise flavored liqueur before, during, and after meals. When ouzo is gifted with the simple kiss of mint, it transforms from frat-house punishment to delightful refreshment.

MAKES

1 ounce ouzo

.5 ounce simple syrup

.25 ounce lemon juice

3 mint leaves

1. Shake and fine strain into a shot glass.

The Mint of Your Enemy's Destruction

When making drinks with shaken mint, remember to fine strain out the little particulates. This keeps bits of torn mint out of the teeth of your friends. However, when serving to enemies, omit the simple syrup and don't fine strain this shot; painful expressions will ensue.

Carthusian Shrub

Plums and cocktails don't really mix. Even the ripest plums must be mashed into oblivion to get any play into a cocktail. The Carthusian Shrub takes fresh plums and roasts out their sweet juices into, well, a shrub. What is a shrub? A type of colonial era, prebottled cocktail consisting of cooked fruit and vinegar. It may sound crazy, but this type of boozy gastrique was a mainstay of drinking culture long before the cocktail was invented.

MAKES

1 de-stoned plum

2 ounces Green Chartreuse

1 ounce water

.25 ounce balsamic vinegar

1. Preheat oven to 350°F.
2. Cover the de-stoned plum with Green Chartreuse, water, and balsamic vinegar in a roasting pan.
3. Roast uncovered for 30 minutes.
4. Allow mixture to cool and strain into a separate vessel.
5. Serve in 1½-ounce shots.
6. Enjoy eating the roasted plum.

Chartreuse: *A Story Better Than a Myth*

A liqueur before it was a color, Chartreuse was fabled to be an elixir for long life. Though the recipe is three hundred years old, the monks who created it have come and gone. Now, only three monks know the recipe at any given time, and they protect it with a vow of silence. All of this sounds like it comes from the world of orcs and elves, but no, it is France.

Hospitality Shot

In its day, there was no sign of luxury and hospitality equal to that of the pineapple. In the modern world of international shipping, most fresh fruits are available throughout the entire world and even the rarest produce is widely available for a minimum of two months at a time. However, shipping a pineapple from the New World back to Europe would have left onlookers agog just five hundred years ago. If you received a pineapple, it showed that no expense was spared. The principal cocktail at that time in history would have been the punch, a five-ingredient mixture of the world's most exotic potables, and that is what the Hospitality Shot is all about.

MAKES

1 ounce genever

.25 ounce lime juice

2 chunks fresh pineapple

1 sprig tarragon

1 pinch curry powder

1. Shake and fine strain into a shot glass.

How Do You Pick a Fresh Pineapple?

The pineapple is a spiky mace of a fruit whose hull will not reveal its secrets. However, its leaves will. You can tell how ripe a pineapple is by gently tugging at a small leaf at the center of the pineapple; the easier it pulls out, the riper the pineapple. If you can lift the pineapple by that one leaf, it is at least one week from being ripe.

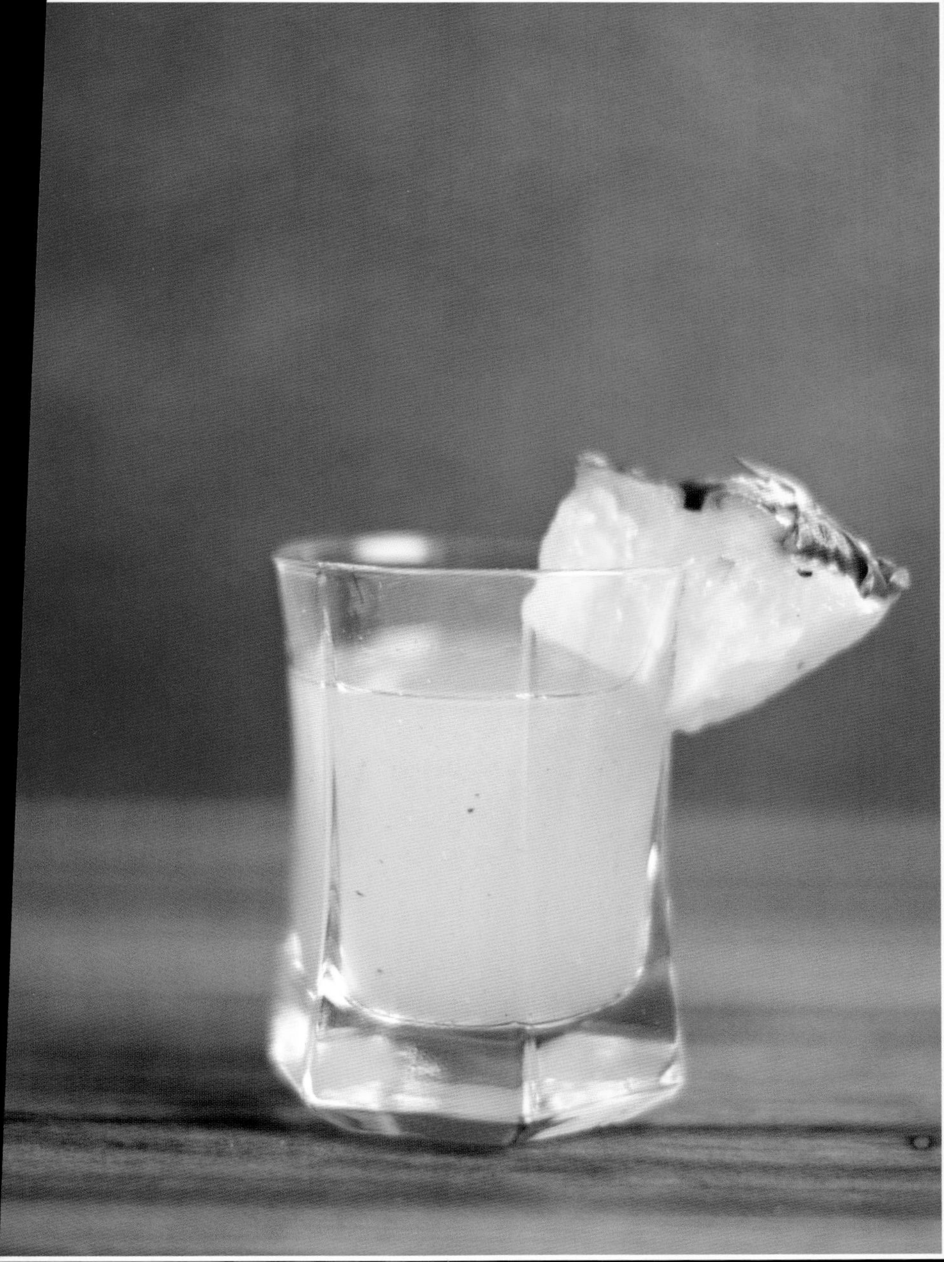

Sorbet Shot

The tiniest strip mall lasagna house still pushes amarone grappa on guests that would rather have a pitcher of pop. Every Italian restaurant has grappa, limoncello, and rosemary, but to quote a famous monorail salesman, "It's like a mule with a spinning wheel. Nobody knows how he got it and danged if he knows how to use it!" Here is how you combine three common ingredients that are either hated, syrupy sweet, or known only as a garnish.

MAKES

.75 ounce grappa

.75 ounce limoncello

1 sprig rosemary

1. Shake and fine strain into a shot glass.

Limoncello: *The Easiest DIY*

Since limoncello is just vodka, sugar, and lemon flavoring, it's easy to make at home. First, buy a bottle of vodka and take two shots. Now there is enough room in the bottle for three whole peels from lemons. Using a Microplane will yield the best results because it avoids the bitter pith, but a peeler will work just fine. Leave the peels in the bottle and refrigerate it. After a week, decant it and mix it with one part simple syrup. Bam, now you're bootlegging!

Grappa: *It's Okay If You Hate It*

Though grappa is not a garbage liquor as many view it, it is a "rustic" spirit. Not rustic like chefs who just use a dull knife, but rustic like un-aged and distilled just once. It isn't for everyone; don't force it.

Mango Fume

It is a very trendy thing in the modern culinary world for chefs to dress up traditional street food and be praised for it. Most tacos are great but street tacos are better. And while there is something special about eating them drunk on the curb, there is also a charm in sitting at a table and having some interesting ingredients, maybe a napkin, and a place to wash your hands. The Mango Fume dresses up a Mexican street snack consisting of diced mango, lime juice, and crushed red pepper. Normally, this treat is served in plastic bags by the side of the road. We'll put it into a glass, but know that authenticity is within your reach.

MAKES

1 ounce tequila

2 (1-inch) chunks mango

.25 ounce lime juice

.25 ounce cream

1 pinch crushed red pepper

1. Muddle the mango chunks in the bottom of a mixing glass.
2. Shake and fine strain into a shot glass.

Dairy, Acid, and Spice

Mixing drinks is a form of cooking—a lazy form that rarely involves heating things. But in mixing drinks, balancing flavor is still the most important measure between good and great. If liquor is a base, then everything else that goes in is situated on the opposite side of an imaginary scale. Acidity (citrus) will balance sweet and spicy. Dairy, eggs, or a neutral fruit add the base and will subtract from spicy, sweet, and acid.

Soft Naga

Pitaya. Sounds adorable, right? The etymology of pitaya, also known as dragon fruit in the United States, comes from several different countries' word for dragon. Ironically, this gentle fruit is a gift from the cactus. To double up on irony, it isn't always an Asian delicacy as most people assume. Dragon fruit varieties are native to South America and Mexico. All of this begs the question, "Why haven't I been drinking dragon fruit Margaritas with my fish tacos?" If you feel robbed by this sudden epiphany, run—don't walk—to the market and start making up for lost time.

MAKES

.75 ounce vodka

.75 ounce blanc vermouth

1 tablespoon dragon fruit

1. Shake and strain into a shot glass.

Blanc Vermouth Is Not Dry, But It Is White

Though *blanc* means *white* and though dry vermouth is white, they are not the same type of wine. The three most common types of vermouth are dry, blanc, and sweet. Dry is the one that is known for its acquaintance with the Martini. Sweet, often called "red," is the vermouth with caramelized sugar that shows up in the Manhattan. Blanc vermouth is another type of sweet vermouth, but it doesn't have caramelized sugar.

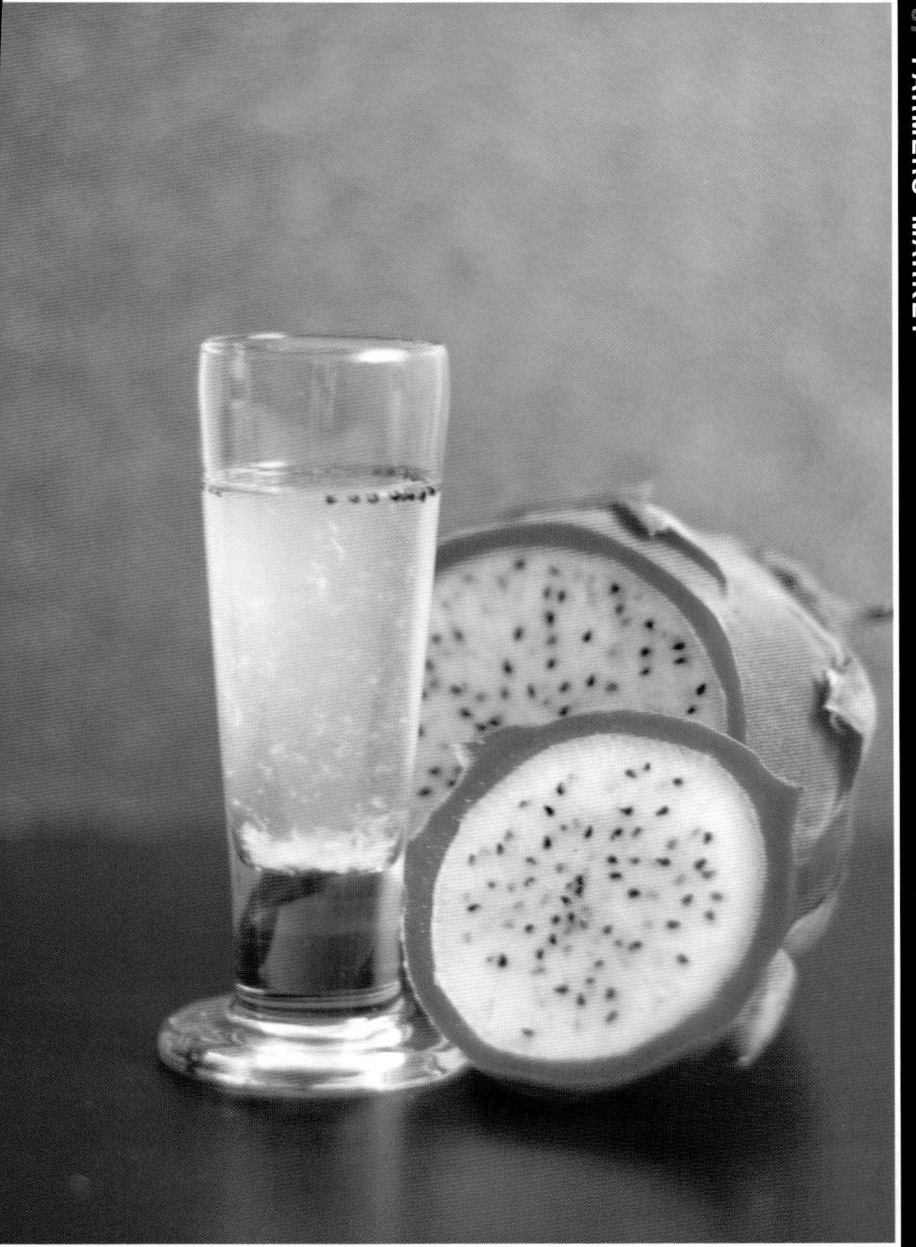

Watermelon Salad

Oftentimes when chefs get into the kitchen they make cocktails like soup. These drinks are abominable and require far too much skill to replicate. However, making a cocktail like a salad works quite well. The combination of watermelon, salt, basil, and fresh feta cheese make a great salad. Drinking cheese is not likely to catch on anytime soon, so we will substitute vodka for that part of the salad. However, serving this shot with a little hunk of feta cheese on the side makes a great party hors d'oeuvre. Garnishing cocktails with cheese is the new sugar rim.

MAKES

1 ounce vodka

2 (1-inch) watermelon cubes

3 basil leaves

1 pinch salt

Feta cheese cube (optional)

1. Shake very hard and fine strain into a shot glass.
2. If brave, garnish with a feta cheese cube.

What Does the Salt Do in a Cocktail?

In most cases, salt will balance acidity and tie flavors together. But in the case of recipes with watermelon, salt balances out the flavor of all of the water in the eponymous melon and brings out the sweetness. Anyone with a Southern drawl will tell you it's true.

Trigger

Roy Rogers has his own gentle mocktail: Coca-Cola and grenadine. The Roy Rogers is supposed to be some sort of masculine version of a Shirley Temple. Roy Rogers may have been the very picture of temperate temperance, but his horse, Trigger, likely had a harder life. This is a simple shot for Trigger. He worked hard, so he gets the whiskey that is left out of Roy's cocktail.

MAKES

3 whole ripe cherries

1.5 ounces bourbon

1. Muddle cherries in a mixing glass.
2. Pour bourbon into the same glass.
3. Shake and fine strain into a shot glass.

Muddler

When using a muddler, remember to gently press down to crush herbs and fruit. There is no need to be sloppy and fast. If you don't feel like splurging on a muddler, you can also use a large wooden spoon. Ideally, you won't be muddling often so it might be fun to search around the house for things you can use as a muddler in a pinch. Remember to keep it gentle though—the gentle hand that you'd use to muddle with an empty glass bottle is the same soft hand you should use with a muddler.

Pick Out Fresh Cherries by Using Your Mouth

It's pretty hard to get a cherry worth eating unless it's between June and September, so let that be your first guide. If you are going to the farmers' market, then anyone will let you try their wares, so taste before you buy. Cherries should be sweet and soft, and they should not require much chewing. Obviously, you should only do this at a farmers' market since eating and spitting cherry seeds could get you kicked out of the grocery store.

Straw-Barrel

Sure, you could leave the rum out of this recipe and have a nice salad dressing, but what's the fun in that? After all, just remember Homer's sage words: "You don't win friends with salad." The balsamic vinegar is the acid in this drink—no lemon or lime needed. Much like a rapper from the 1990s, Jamaican rum is funky and fresh and will pair with the fruit flavors well. The Straw-Barrel shot is all about growing one's palate. Rum and strawberries? That is child's play. The tannins from balsamic vinegar add character to the shot, and the black pepper is a final frontier for drinking, so hold the hand of someone you love and take your first step across the bridge of "flavor pairings."

MAKES

1 hulled strawberry

.5 ounce balsamic vinegar

1 ounce Jamaican rum

1 pinch ground black pepper

2 basil leaves

1. Muddle the strawberries and basil with the balsamic vinegar. Then add the Jamaican rum and a pinch of pepper.
2. Shake and fine strain into a shot glass.

Strawberries: *The Quirky Ingredient*

Fresh strawberries or any fresh berries are tricky little devils in drinks. If the fruit isn't ripe enough, it will only add acidity to your cocktail. If the strawberries you picked out are a little on the tart side, just add a touch of sugar to them before using them in this recipe.

Spa Water

Cucumbers in cocktails became popular in the early 2000s, but cucumbers in actual booze bottles have yet to have their day. The Spa Water shot is a great way to be able to serve shots to a large party with very low effort. A low effort to high payoff reward isn't the high road, but it is an easy way to bank a few compliments. Assemble the following recipe into whatever pouring device you need or use Mason jar technology.

MAKES

1 bottle vodka

1 cucumber split lengthwise 4 times

4 sprigs mint

4 sprigs tarragon

6 ounces water

2 whole lemon peels

1. Combine ingredients in a bottle or Mason jar.
2. Refrigerate for 24 hours.
3. Serve 1.5 ounces to a shot.

Infusions Without the Bitterness of Botulism

Ever see those big jars of fruit and spices "infusing" on a bar in a restaurant? Gross, disgusting, and in many states, now illegal. The problem with these infusions is that bars don't know how to infuse spirits. When left out at room temperature, the flavors fade away and the perishable ingredients like fruits or vegetables go bad. You need to stick to three rules when infusing alcohol: (1) make sure there's a need for the infusion; (2) keep it in your fridge; (3) remember that they don't take longer than a day or two (hard spices may take up to five days).

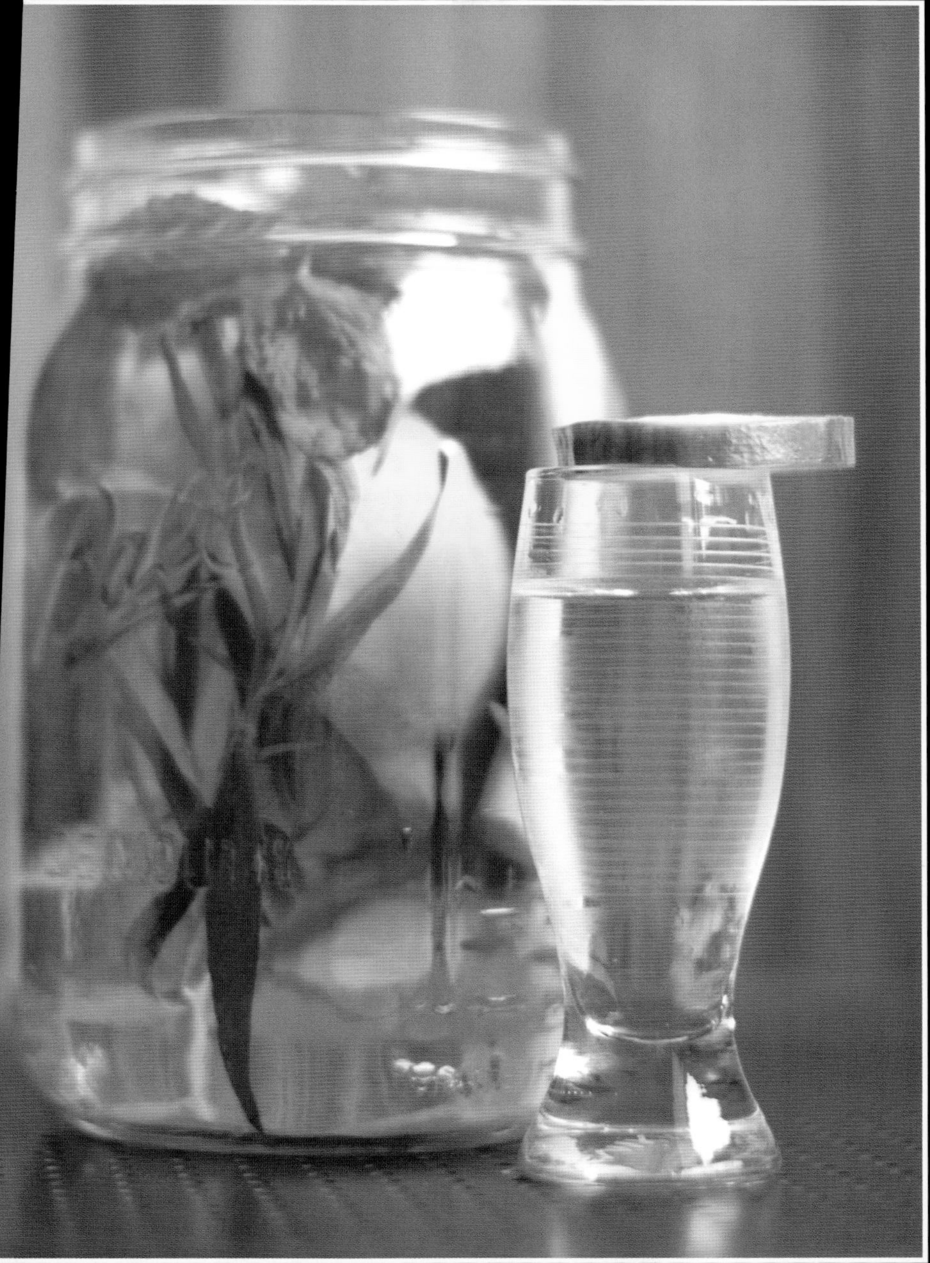

Blackberry Boo Boo

The Blackberry Boo Boo is another tribute to underrated sidekicks. Without Boo Boo, Yogi would just be a giant idiot running all over the place and causing a ruckus; you need a little ego to balance that. Boo Boo's shot will be a delicate treat as opposed to devouring a pick-a-nick basket whole.

MAKES

1 ounce cognac

3 ripe blackberries

.5 ounce honey syrup

2 dashes Peychaud's bitters

1. Shake and fine strain into a shot glass.

Honey Syrup: *An Easier Way to Make Cocktails*

Honey is difficult to measure in cocktails and sometimes too thick. To transform honey into honey syrup, simply add one part warm water to one part honey. Note that when honey is diluted it is easier to work with, but you will also have to use it all within two weeks.

Blueberry Bruiser

Perhaps this shot should be called the trust tree. In actuality blueberry and fennel flavors team up so much it's surprising that there hasn't been some sort of buddy comedy made about them. That would, however, only work as a fiercely esoteric children's cartoon. Anyway, blueberry and fennel are a culinary duo that show up in ice cream, soup, salad, and now shots. This shot calls for fennel leaves only, but you can easily find a use for the whole plant.

MAKES

1.5 ounces gin

1 sizeable stem of fennel leaves

5 ripe blueberries

1. Shake very hard and fine strain into a shot glass.

Shouldn't I Have Muddled the Fennel?

Sure, if you want to work harder and not smarter. Ripe blueberries should be so soft that they are hard to handle. And fennel leaves will easily be bruised (get it?) by the ice in your new very-hard-shaking technique. However, fine straining though a mesh strainer is essential lest you desire a chunky style shot.

Can't Find Fresh Fennel Leaves?

Use a pinch of Chinese five-spice power. Fennel is a primary flavor in that.

Rhubarb Blossom

Everyone's fat auntie is also trying to buy up all the rhubarb and bake a million pies. Don't stop them—those pies are great—but save some of that rhubarb for drinking too. It is a terrible secret to tell, but pie filling is a culinary clutch tantamount to reducing mushroom soup (it always works) to make a lovely steak sauce. The basic principle is that any pie will function as a shot too. But the rhubarb rouser has a subtle secret that pies can't steal: crème du violet. This delicate liqueur will bring a floral note that no pie can match.

MAKES

1 ounce light rum

.5 ounce rhubarb compote

.25 ounce crème du violet

1. Shake and fine strain into a shot glass.

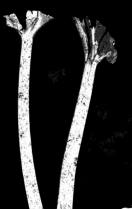

Don't See Rhubarb Compote in the Store?

You'll have a hard time finding rhubarb compote in the store because that would be like seeing tap water on the shelves. Dice up about 4 stalks of rhubarb and boil them in just enough water to cover them. Dissolve 1 cup of sugar into the mix, and if you want an extra touch of flavor, throw a whole vanilla bean in there too. When you are done, you'll have a compote great for ice cream, snacking, or boozing.

Fruit-loupe

Even though cantaloupe is often confined to insipid supermarket fruit platters, it has potential to be good. When it's fresh and not precut, drying under cellophane, it can be magic. Peruvian pisco is a type of brandy that is distilled once and un-aged. It is a spicy, potent, and complex spirit that can stand up to anything. Other spirits would be trampled by the duo of juicy cantaloupe and Irish cream liqueur.

MAKES

1 ounce Peruvian pisco

.5 ounce Baileys

3 (1-inch) cantaloupe cubes

1 pinch of salt

1. Refrigerate all ingredients overnight to get them cold.
2. Blend ingredients using an emersion blender or a counter-top blender and pour into a shot glass.

Blender, WTF?

Truth be told, asking for a blended drink is like asking for one's binky. Blended drinks are perfectly legitimate, but there are a couple of rules to remember. If you're not using ice, like in this recipe, thoroughly chill all ingredients. When using ice, always use exactly as much ice as liquid and plan on sweetening the drink; blended ice dilutes sweetness away.

Baileys: *That's Not Really Milk, Right?*

Baileys is indeed a low-alcohol, shelf-stable whiskey, sugar, and dairy product. It will go bad about one year after opening, so keep your coffee lightly spiked.

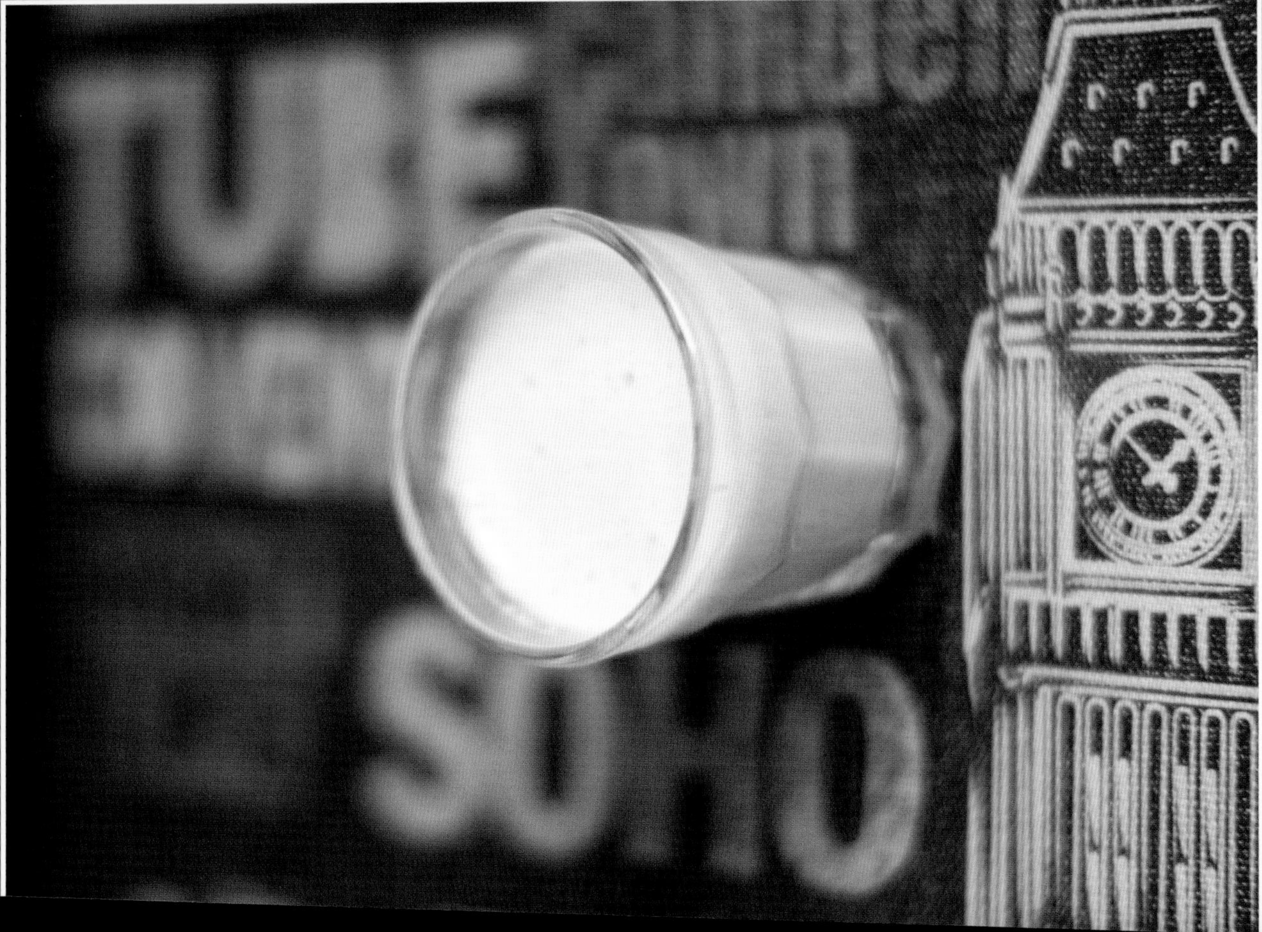

Sagebrush Shot

Sage and ginger aren't a very common pair. However, the ginger rhizome (a root cluster, and a powerful player on the Scrabble board) and the sage leaf do share mutual friends. Ginger's spicy side is mellowed in a classic lime juice, gin, and ginger ale combo called a Dragonfly. Sage adds a savory note that really brings the whole shot together.

MAKES

1 ounce gin

.5 ounce ginger liqueur

.25 ounce fresh lime

4 sage leaves

1. Shake and fine strain into a shot glass.

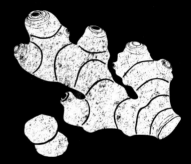

Ginger Liqueur: *It's a Bit of a Racket*

Ginger liqueur doesn't exactly come cheap, though there is no reason why it shouldn't. In the absence of ginger liqueur, you could make this same shot by muddling a bit of peeled ginger with a touch of sugar. Remember that the easiest way to peel ginger is just to use the humble spoon. Scraping a spoon across a ginger root will clean it up in no time.

Milky Joe

Coconut might not be at your average farmers' market, but it is generally found fresh year round at the grocery store since it's pretty much just fruit encased in wood. The idea behind the Milky Joe is as simple as creating a fresh Piña Colada that doesn't require a blender. If you can't find a coconut, canned coconut water is an acceptable substitute. The fresh flavors of cachaça will spike this shot up and make it great for the beach or the patio. This shot was created by Jamie Boudreau, a Canadian.

MAKES

1 ounce cachaça

.75 ounce coconut water

.25 ounce fresh lime or
   a squeeze from 1 lime

1. Shake and strain into a shot glass.

Cachaça: *How to Say It and What It Is*

First: Kuh-Shatt-suh. Not too hard. Cachaca is like rum (and some say it predates rum), but is made from a single distillation of fresh-pressed sugar cane. The result is more floral, rich, and fresh tasting. It is the national spirit of Brazil and ranges (in Brazil) from might-as-well-be-gasoline to artesian spirit. There are a few on the market in the United States, so do a quick Internet search and read reviews to see which brands are awful and which are amazing. And remember, great ones can still cost less than $30 a bottle.

Devil's Avocado

It isn't exactly fair for so many tequila cocktails to be named for demons and devils, but puns cannot be walked away from so easily. The avocado is a buttery little devil that's as luxurious as sushi. Personal wealth and worth should be measured by how often one can involve avocados in one's life.

MAKES

1 ounce tequila

⅛ of an avocado

4 leaves cilantro

.25 ounce lime juice

.25 ounce simple syrup

1 pinch crushed red pepper

1. Refrigerate all ingredients overnight to get them cold.

2. Remove ingredients from refrigerator, blend using an emersion blender or a counter-top blender, and pour into a shot glass.

The Avocado Handshake

Make sure you feel your avocado before purchasing it. Unripe avocados could be slung at Goliath's head for a deathblow. Avocados that are overripe will move under the fruit's skin. Perfectly ripe avocados will feel like the palm of your hand.

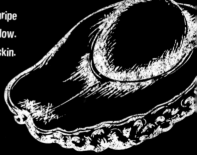

Liquid Wetsuit

The idea of the wetsuit is to keep you warm using your own body heat—and nothing will warm a body like green Chartreuse. However, green Chartreuse doesn't really have a reputation as a surfing, beach-going partier. Luckily, Chartreuse has an amazing partner in pineapple juice. Though they come from different worlds, they pair together perfectly.

MAKES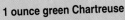

1 ounce green Chartreuse

1 ounce pineapple juice

1. Shake and fine strain into a shot glass.

Warming Chartreuse

Chartreuse packs a punch. It is a liqueur that still maintains a proof of 110. The sugar might cover the burn of the booze, but the herbal warmth of the elixir will wash over you like sunshine. The recipe was perfected more than 300 years ago by the Carthusian monk Brother Gerome. Brother Gerome used Chartreuse for medicine, and placebo or not, it does make you feel better.

Part 4

HOLIDAYS

People have often said that Repeal Day, which happens on December 5 and is the anniversary of the repeal of American prohibition, is the only real drinking holiday. While Repeal Day certainly offers a perfect reason for drinking, there are plenty of other holidays that can't be holidays without drinking. This is another reason why we always forget Arbor Day until it creeps up on us. Solemnly observing Ireland's exile of serpents is boring, but getting drunk in mid March is a treat. Every holiday needs a shot, and these shots are great for getting into the spirit at office parties or for ditching work and packing a flask.

Buddha's New Year

The beginning of each new year is a time for rebirth. Buddha's New Year shot will help you with that transition into a new life. In the winter months we are occasionally blessed with a truly bizarre ethereal fruit from Southeast Asia. The Buddha's hand is a yellow citrus fruit that has a flesh indiscernible from its pith. It doesn't really have much of a taste, but its entrancing scent is so complex that it cannot be described. To enjoy this in a cocktail, it must be infused.

MAKES

1 ounce infused Buddha's hand vodka

.5 ounce Benedictine

1. Stir and strain into a shot glass.

A Shot for Rebirth

The Buddha's hand fruit is uniquely delicate. It is also uniquely light in acidity and bitterness. It is a citrus fruit soft and mild enough to eat the skin and flesh without processing it. To best capture the spirit of this fruit, use a vegetable peeler to slice the Buddha's hand into wafer-thin slices and mix in an equal part spirit by volume. Think of it just like peeling a potato except instead of turning the fruit, you'll continue cutting into it with the peeler until it's sliced up thin like deli meat. Buddha's hand has almost no bitterness, so it can easily infuse for one week without taking on any bitter qualities.

Wind Beneath My Wings

Scotch is the most coveted booze there is. Like a man struck by Cupid's arrow, Scotch aficionados will tell you at great length of their love for the barley-based product. However, what these folks often forget is another cliché: Behind every great man is a great woman. The great "woman" behind Scotch is sherry. Scotch is rarely ever aged in new barrels, and many of the most prized bottles are nurtured from old sherry barrels. The Wind Beneath My Wings celebrates this lop-sided partnership.

MAKES

1 ounce single malt Scotch

.5 ounce Pedro Ximénez sherry

1 lemon twist

1. Stir and strain into a shot glass.
2. Garnish with a lemon twist.

The Lemon Twist as a Third Ingredient

The lemon twist is not only placed in a cocktail to make it pretty, but it also adds aroma and acidity. The citric oils in the zest, if sprayed directly on the glass, greatly change the flavor of the cocktail. The actual zest itself doesn't even need to be in the cocktail.

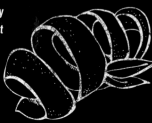

Perfect Love

The central ingredient in the Perfect Love shot is parfait amour. It is a vibrant blue curaçao-based liqueur flavored with almond, rose petals, and vanilla. Yes, it turns out you really can get all things sexy in one bottle. The mythos of parfait amour is that lovers are to share a glass over ice and forever be in love. At the time of the cocktail's invention, ice would have been the height of luxury. This recipe serves to update parfait amour's use as a Valentine's Day standard.

MAKES

.5 ounce parfait amour

.5 ounce vodka

.5 ounce fino sherry

1. Stir and strain into a shot glass.

Balancing a Perfect Love

Fino sherry is drunk by the brave with cured meats or used for cooking and forgotten about in dusty pantries. It is also used to add acidity to cocktails. Though fino sherry is quite pungent on its own, it combines nicely with the richness and smooth grace of parfait amour.

Dollar Bill

President's Day is pretty lame, but who can complain when you get paid to spend the day doing nothing but drinking? Let's call it what it is: Bank Holiday Monday, a perfect time to celebrate with a drink. The Dollar Bill is a cocktail that pays homage to our founding fathers' drinking style. Even better than having a shot or two of the ol' Dollar Bill, get twisted on a slew of them and then go out mattress or carpet shopping. Give those retailers what they're looking for! The Dollar Bill also has a diplomacy about it that makes it enjoyable for all.

MAKES

1 ounce applejack

.5 ounce pineapple juice

.5 ounce cranberry juice

.5 ounce blackstrap dark rum

1. Shake and fine strain into a shot glass.

Applejack: *An American Mongrel Spirit*

Applejack was originally made by freezing hard cider, removing ice, and enjoying the resulting higher proof spirit. This process is called *jacking*, and it is also known as the *Mongolian still*. This process of frozen distillation doesn't allow for the removal of unpleasant or toxic elements. Applejack is no longer made this way, and these days it is defined as an American, 51% apple-based (minimum) spirit.

I Shot the Caesar

Shortly before St. Patrick's Day there is a little known Canadian holiday called the Ides of March. The lack of knowledge about this holiday's existence is mostly due to the fact that it is made up. The customs of the North-men are strange. Every March 15 brings a day when the fur traders of the constitutional monarchy to the North drink blended tomatoes and clam juice. The best anthropologists of the United States have yet to determine the source of this custom.

MAKES

1 ounce vodka

.5 ounce Clamato juice

1 dash hot sauce

1. Gently shake and strain into a salt-rimmed shot glass.

Clamato Juice

Clamato juice is a drink made from tomato juice and clam broth. In defiance of all reason, it is actually pleasant in flavor. It is the signature ingredient of the Bloody Caesar, which is Canada's favorite beverage (after beer, of course). The Bloody Caesar is far superior to the Bloody Mary for the addition of the umami flavor gifted from the noble clam.

St. Patrick's Shroud

Nobody really knows who St. Patrick was, why he was canonized, or why we celebrate St. Patrick's Day. St. Patrick was best known for driving the (nonexistent) snakes out of Ireland. There are two ways to think of this man: Either he was a good man whom we know nothing about or he was secretly a huge fan of parades and public drinking. The general pattern of history tells us that the truth often lies somewhere in the middle.

MAKES

1 ounce Irish whiskey

.5 ounce dry vermouth

1 dash crème de menthe

1. Stir and strain into a shot glass.

Irish Whiskey

Irish whiskey is made from grains and must be aged in wooden barrels for three years. If it's blended whiskey, the bottle must say "blended whiskey." These minimalistic rules easily make Irish whiskey the least defined, most diverse, and fully "shrouded in mystery" spirit. In general, Irish whiskey is a lighter-style, more subtle whiskey.

The Internet Shot

April Fools' Day has been solidly appropriated by the Internet. If you believe that Chaucer's Canterbury Tales was the first record of an April Fools' Day, then it squarely took seven hundred years for the Internet to own it. In 2005, a fake BBC web page reported that in a Cambodian government-sanctioned battle, an African lion fought and mutilated forty-two midgets in a ring fight. And since then, that great day in prankster history, the Internet has owned April Fools' Day. The Internet Shot pays homage to the most humorous of days: April Fools'. It is a crystal clear shot with a flavor that will be unknown to its drinkers. The server of this shot could say the ingredients are anything between tap water to distiller albino maple syrup.

MAKES

1 ounce slivovitz

.25 ounce gin

.25 ounce simple syrup

1. Stir and strain into a shot glass.

Slivovitz

Slivovitz is a traditional, artisan spirit from Croatia made from blue plums. Slivovitz is most commonly called for as an ice cold shot. It is what is called an *eau-de-vie*, a brandy made from just one type of fruit (plums in this case), un-aged and unsweetened. Any *eau-de-vie* basically tastes of a bone-dry version of the fruit that it is made of.

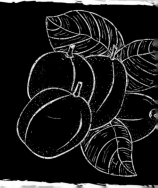

Cinco de Ignacio

Everyone knows that May 5 is the day of the year when we celebrate General Ignacio Zaragoza Seguín's victory over French forces at the Battle of Puebla on May 5, 1862. Right? Everyone knows that? Mexico actually became independent on September 16, 1810. Much like the complete lack of understanding of St. Patrick's Day, Cinco de Mayo might as well just keep rolling as a massive drinking holiday.

MAKES

1 ounce mezcal

.5 ounce lager

.25 ounce lime juice

2 dashes orange bitters

1 pinch salt

1. Stir and strain into a shot glass.

Mezcal

All tequila is a type of mezcal. The easiest way to think of mezcal is this: Tequila is a more specific and refined version of this rustic spirit. Tequila was legally defined seven-eighths of the way into the Mexican government's history. Yes, in 1984, tequila reluctantly got some rules. Much like bourbon, tequila's history went back a few hundred years and was governed by tradition and not by law nor appellation. Now, tequila can only be created in five Mexican states and be made from Blue Webber agave. Mezcal, however, can be made anywhere in Mexico and from twenty-eight recognized varieties of agave. Most of the mezcal you'll see in the export market though is from the state of Oaxaca and made from Espadin agave.

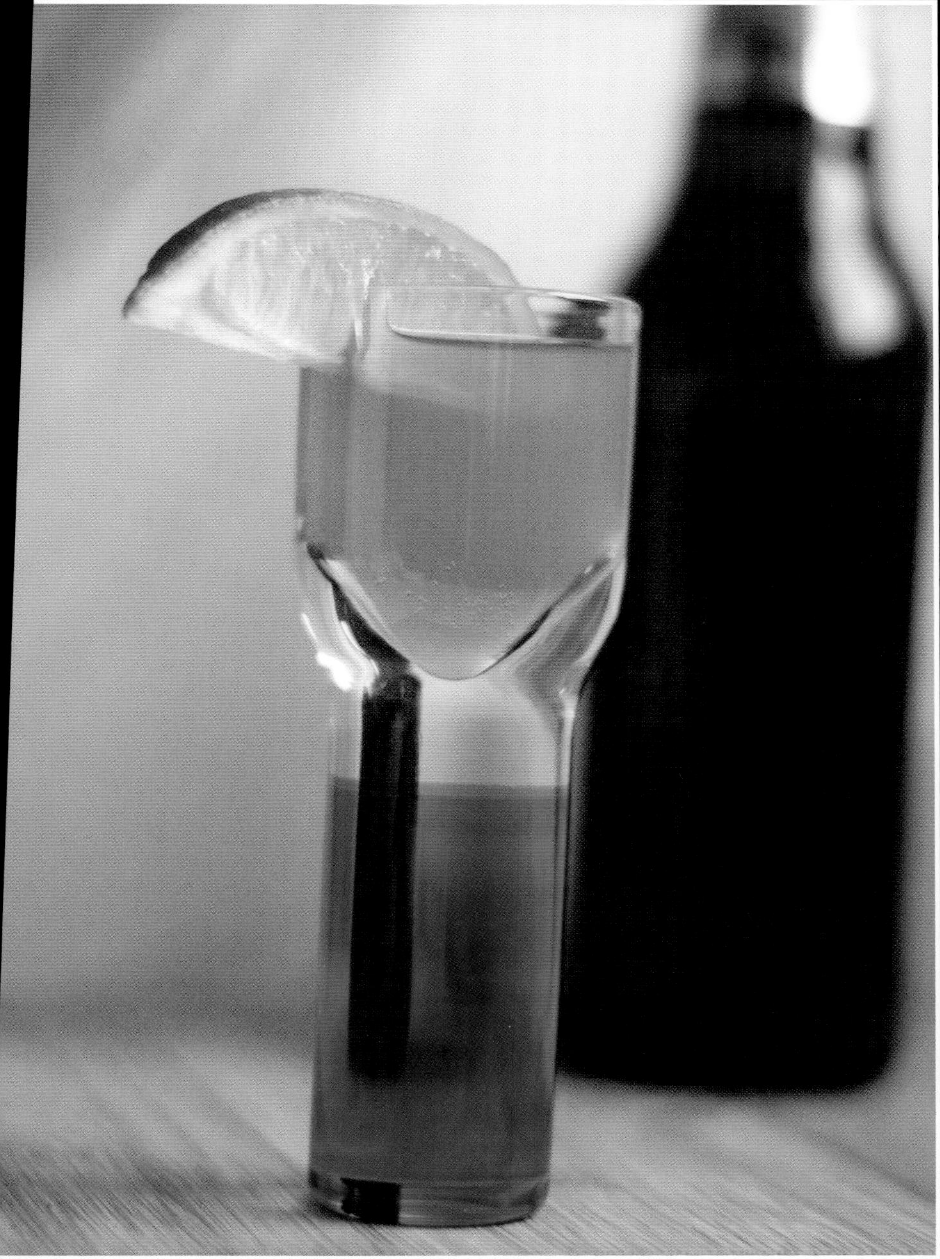

Stonewall Shot

There are a few cocktails out there that go by the name of Stonewall, but they all draw influence from an eccentric general rather than the last week in June. Gay pride deserves a cocktail, and perhaps the Stonewall is that shot. The Stonewall is named for the Stonewall Bar, a little joint in Greenwich Village that, during the last week in June 1969, became a landmark battleground for gay rights.

MAKES

.75 ounce rye whiskey

.75 ounce elderflower liqueur

1 dash Angostura bitters

1 dash Peychaud's bitters

1. Stir and strain into a shot glass.

New York: *A City Filled with Cocktails*

Everyone knows the Manhattan, but almost every little nook in New York has a Manhattan-ish cocktail named for it. The next two best-known classics would be the gin-based Bronx and the rye-based Brooklyn. A couple of modern versions include the Greenpoint and the Redhook.

Canadian Whisky vs. Rye Whiskey

First off, Canada has no *e* in *whisky*. Second, American rye whiskey has a base of 51% rye, while the opposite is true of Canadian whisky. Canadian whisky is at least 51% neutral grain spirit with the remainder being any type of whisky; in the modern world, it is mostly corn.

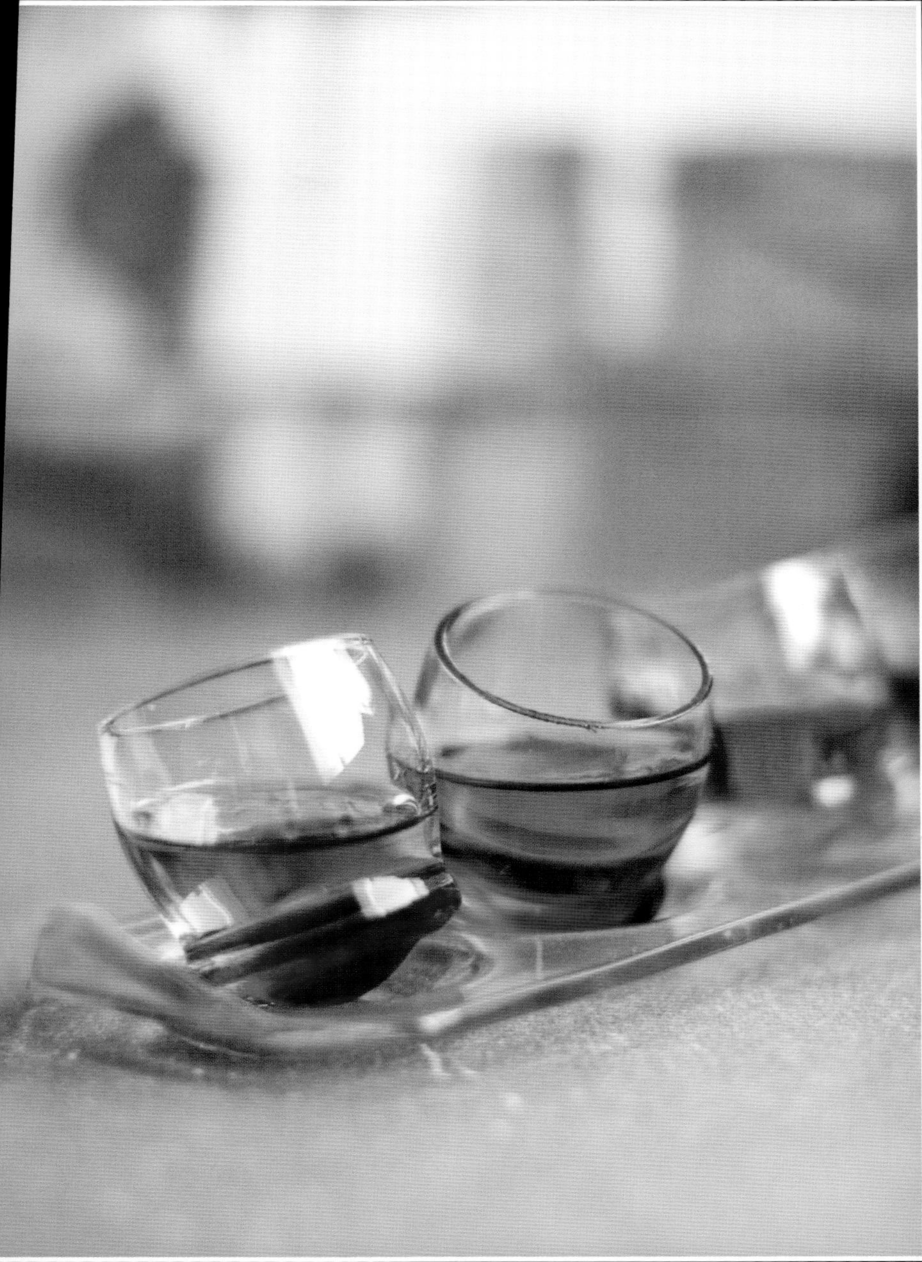

The **Dread Pirate Dave**

Talk Like a Pirate Day happens every year on September 19, but it wasn't until Dave Barry featured it in a column in 2002 that it really took off. And like every real holiday, it needs its own cocktail. John Baur and Mark Summers began talking like pirates back in 1995, and now they will finally get their rum. The Dread Pirate Dave shot is lightly inspired by a grog-like drink, even though that dram was invented long after the heyday of the pirate.

MAKES

1 ounce spiced rum

.5 ounce cider

.25 ounce lime juice

2 slices muddled ginger

1. Shake and fine strain into a vessel that you have stolen.

Spiced Rum

Though there are many spiced rums out there, it is sometimes difficult to find a great rum because they are hidden behind bolder, bigger brands of rum. Make sure you check out the shelf before going with the usual; you'll be surprised by what you'll find. It's also easy to make your own spiced rum. To make a quality pirate potable, grab a bottle of pedestrian rum and add ten cloves and a stick of cinnamon. Let the mix soak for a week and you'll never have to worry about the rum being all gone again!

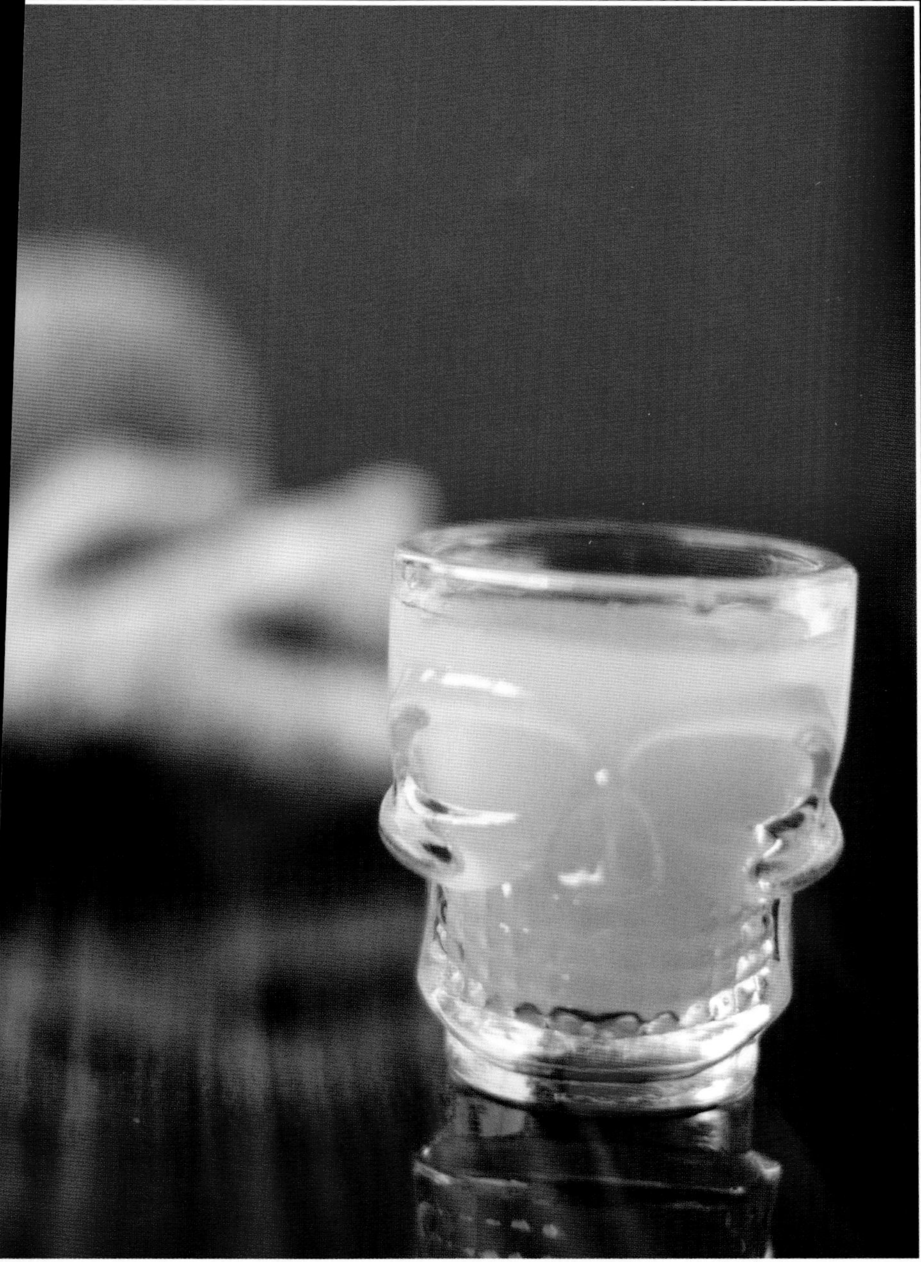

Cocoa Muerto

November's Day of the Dead isn't really a drinking holiday yet, but many tequila companies have begun to see that they can stretch out Halloween parties for up to a week if the calendar works out correctly. The Coco Muerto blends the spice of tequila, the herbal quality of sweet vermouth, and the rich velvet of drinking chocolate.

MAKES

.5 ounce tequila

.5 ounce sweet vermouth

1 ounce drinking chocolate

1 pinch cinnamon

1. Stir and strain first three ingredients into a shot glass.

2. Garnish with cinnamon on top.

Drinking Chocolate vs. Hot Cocoa

Drinking chocolate is made from chocolate, and hot chocolate is actually made from cocoa powder. To explain that further, cocoa powder is roasted chocolate from which the fat has been removed. Keeping the fat in drinking chocolate is what makes it so rich and smooth, even when diluted with an ounce of booze.

Sicilian

Blood orange is the best flavor of winter. This syrupy, bittersweet orange is the primary orange grown in all of Italy. The blood orange's legend ties into the blood spilled in the world of organized crime, which is where the name for this shot comes from. Those who have worked with blood orange at great length will testify to the danger of the blood orange staining one's clothes. These fruits make spots that no dry cleaner can put asunder.

MAKES

1 ounce grappa

.5 ounce sweet vermouth

.5 ounce blood orange

1. Shake and strain into a shot glass.

Grappa in Cocktails

Grappa can be a bit tough, but keep in mind that there are as many types of grappa as there are wines. Lighter grappas will have a tendency to have more high-end astringent notes. The heavier grappas will provide more round flavors and some, such as amarone, will really make beautiful, full-flavored cocktails.

Blitzen

Sure, everyone knows the story of Rudolph. But while that story is great around the holidays, he certainly was a one-note wonder. And the rest of those reindeers? They're more of a beer and wine crowd—not much to write about. Yet Blitzen's story as a reindeer was terribly underrated. Most people don't know it, but Blitzen always carried a flask. Now, there's a reindeer who knows how to live.

MAKES

1 ounce cognac

.75 ounce cranberry juice

.25 ounce Angostura bitters

1. Stir and strain into a shot glass.

Bitters as a Digestive Aid

Adding large amounts of bitters to cocktails is very trendy these days. It makes big flavors happen and truly confuses the palate in amazing ways. However, people often forget that bitters were originally used as a digestive aid, and that drinking too many too quickly can cause quick digestion. Drinking too much absinthe makes you a better painter, drinking too much tequila can get you in a fight, and drinking too many bitters can have you running for the bathroom.

Gelt

The Gelt shot is based on small chocolate gold coins given during the Hanukkah season. Gelt is for every adult who loves chocolate, shots, and an eight-day celebration.

MAKES

1 ounce red wine

.25 ounce crème de cacao

.25 ounce cinnamon schnapps

1. Stir and strain into a shot glass.

What Are Schnapps?

In Europe, schnapps were a specific high-proof distilled spirit bone-dry that tasted only of what they were named for. Americans took the word *schnapps* and added massive amounts of sugar and other flavors to the bottle.

Cinnamon Schnapps

When it comes to cinnamon schnapps, you'll find that any brand will do, but you should keep a few things in mind. Mainly, there is no reason for this spirit to have any color, so if it comes out candy apple red, that is a bad sign. There are a few good ones on the market, and they're also well known as ingredients for shooters. You've probably heard of a good one that has little flakes of gold in the bottle.

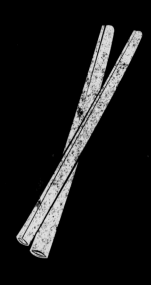

Umoja

Umoja is Kwanzaa's word for unity. The Umoja shot represents ingredients from all over the world. Apples began in Central Asia and traveled the entire world; port's very name comes from travel; cane-based rum is now made the world over; and the corn from bourbon is the world's most harvested crop. A touch of Darjeeling tea adds a little bit of bitterness from India and mellows the sweetness of the other ingredients.

MAKES

.5 ounce bourbon

.5 ounce rum

.5 ounce apple juice

.5 ounce port

.5 ounce Darjeeling tea

1. Shake and stain into a shot glass.

Port: *Is That Forty-Year-Old Wine?*

The age noted on a bottle of booze denotes a minimum age of all spirits in the bottle. The age noted on port means the exact inverse. A forty-year-old port will contain at least some wine that has made it to the year listed.

Part 5

DESSERT &
AFTER
DINNER

n between pirates taking gulps of rum and college kids doing body shots, there was a very straightforward purpose for shots: after-dinner drinks. In some cases, as in the bitter digestivos of Italy and France or the dry schnapps of Germany, these were thrown down after a meal for a happy stomach and a mellow buzz. These bitter and dry shots are for bitter and dry people and are not really crowd pleasers. Later in the history of cocktails, the layered shot became a delicate delicacy. These shots, which are called *pousse-cafés*, were meant to have each layer gingerly sipped after dinner. In the 1970s, the rise in popularity of the B-52 brought back the pousse-café. These drinks will work best if the booze is refrigerated and slowly poured over a spoon. Or you can do it the way that bartenders were taught in the 1970s: Pour the liquor slowly over a cherry to achieve the layered effect. Dessert shots are also the perfect substitute for sugary cocktails—of which no sensible person would want a full serving. These dessert shots are more about replacing dessert than pairing with dessert.

Madre Sucia

The lowest effort and highest reward pousse-café you can make is the Madre Sucia. In English it means "dirty mother," an awful cocktail from the 1970s that combines brandy, coffee liqueur, and ice. Although brandy and coffee liqueur don't quite go well together, dark coffee liqueur with a fine tequila layered on top of it is indeed a treat. Coffee and tequila are quite a natural pair, so much so that many small tequila distilleries have a house coffee liqueur brand. In the past the coffee liqueur of choice would have been Kahlúa, which is a great product, but these days there are many other options. Kahlúa Especial is one to try because it has double the booze of regular Kahlúa and much more flavor. Patron XO, which is 80 proof and caffeinated, and Fair Café, a fair trade coffee liqueur, are also good brands to try.

MAKES

.5 ounce coffee liqueur, chilled

.5 ounce reposado tequila, chilled

1. In order, slowly pour each refrigerated ingredient into a shot glass.

How Do I Pick a Tequila?

Tequila only has to be 51% agave by law, but that is a pass/fail attitude. In the modern world you can often buy 100% agave for $20 a bottle. After you've upgraded that part of your liquor cabinet, pick a tequila that you like. Tequila runs the gamut from sweet and floral to gritty and fierce. Try a few at your local taqueria to find the right one. No local taqueria? Move to a new town.

Ginger Snap

Cocktail enthusiasts will often say that drinks should not taste like childhood flavors to cover up the taste of alcohol. While this is true to understand alcohol, once you transcend that understanding, you'll find that drinking your favorite dessert is quite enjoyable, and nearly every cookie in the jar can be represented with alcohol. The Ginger Snap is one that will hopefully take you back to after-school moments with your hand in the cookie jar—with the welcome addition of rum.

MAKES

1 ounce black strap rum

.25 ounce simple syrup

.25 ounce lime juice

2 dashes Angostura bitters

1. Shake and strain into a shot glass.

Black Strap Rum

Black strap rum is not necessarily distilled from black strap molasses. Often, it is very, very dark rum that is flavored to taste like black strap molasses. Do not be disheartened by this deceit; it still adds amazing depth of flavor to cocktails, baked goods, and piracy.

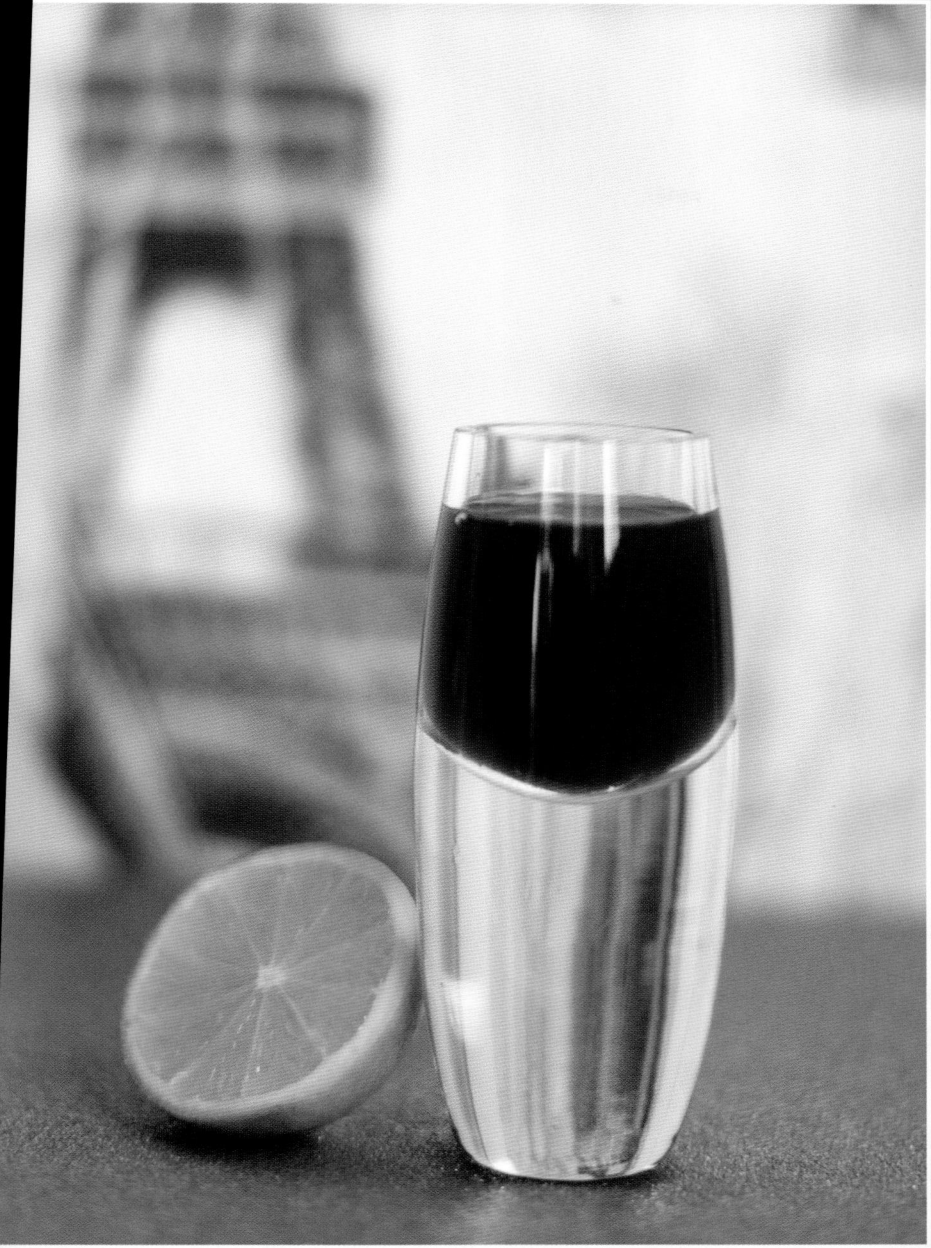

Root Beer Slammer

Be careful of the Root Beer Slammer, for it will taste like you're just drinking right from the soda fountain. Over 100 years ago, when pharmacists would make tonics from extracts, roots, and potions, the world clearly was more enjoyable. That was a world in which a pharmacist could manufacture Coca-Cola in the back room. And it was a world where the distillers' tools were almost identical to those of the pharmacist. The Root Beer Slammer reunites those trades again, creating a flavor that is so complex and amazing that even a child who loves root beer could enjoy it. But if you start doing shots with children, expect a call from CPS and save up for lawyer bills.

MAKES

.75 ounce Galliano, chilled

.75 ounce Coca-Cola, chilled

1. Pour ingredients together into a shot glass and slam.

Hecho en Mexico

Mexican Coke is quite popular these days. It is not because of some secret ingredient that they add to it but because of the secret ingredient they don't add to it. Coca-Cola manufactured in America is full of corn syrup. While Coke tastes differently all around the world, corn syrup is not a legal additive in many parts of the world. Taste the difference for yourself.

The Beauteous Daughter

Hopefully this next shot sounds confusing, because it is. It should set you back just as much as when an elderly person says, "She is a handsome woman." This one is from the confusing palate of author A. J. Rathbun. It contains not just one but two bizarre ingredients. The first is genever, the most ancient style of pre-gin. The other is Cardamaro, an Italian wine-based artichoke bitter liqueur. The combination of the two will give you a rich, bittersweet veggie shot—perfect to confuse one's palate right after dinner.

MAKES

.75 ounce genever

.5 ounce Cardamaro Amaro

.25 ounce simple syrup

2 dashes Regan's orange bitters

1 lemon twist

1. Stir and strain first four ingredients into a shot glass. Garnish with a lemon twist.

Genever

Most liquor today has a reputation that prevents people from just shooting it. However, with genever, that is the tradition. Not only is it intended to be gulped down, but it is also used as a beer chaser. Traditionally, one bends at the waist, all the way over, and slurps the genever out of a small tulip glass. This is called the *kopstoot*—or, in English, *head butt*.

Vanilla Nut Passion

Vanilla Nut Passion is not a failed Ben & Jerry's flavor. It is actually too subtle for them. This shot combines hazelnut, vanilla, and passion fruit into a flavor combination that rarely leaves cream puff stores in Hawaii, until now. Passion fruit can often be hard to find, but remember that Lilikoi is the same thing.

MAKES

1 ounce Tuaca

.5 ounce passion fruit puree

.25 ounce simple syrup

1 mint leaf

1. Shake and strain first three ingredients into a shot glass. Garnish with a mint leaf.

Passion Fruit: *It's Kind of a Flavorful Lemon*

Passion fruit shows up mostly in pastries and juice cocktails, so many people don't know how acidic it is. Passion fruit puree by itself will have an acidity almost on par with the lemon and will almost always need to be sweetened up. The upside is that the sugar will help preserve the puree.

Tuaca

Tuaca is another traditional and unique liqueur of Italy. It doesn't show up in many classic cocktails because it wasn't exported to America until after WWII. It basically came over with pizza. Tuaca's flavor is a subtle blend of hazelnut and vanilla—unlike its competitors, which are more like artificially flavored IHOP pancake syrup.

Cachaça Foster

When it comes to bananas, you need to either use baby food to make cocktails or buck up and get a blender. If you're blending bananas, take this tip from a baker: Let them go brown and then freeze them. The concentrated sugar of a brown banana is perfect for blending or for bread. But that isn't all that is interesting about the Cachaça Foster; this shot has fire to top it all off. Enjoy and take care.

MAKES

1.5 ounces cachaça

½ banana

.5 ounce cream

1 teaspoon sugar

2 dashes 151 proof rum

1. Put first three ingredients into blender and top with just enough ice to cover the fluid. Blend until smooth.

2. Strain into a shot glass.

3. Sprinkle the shot glass with sugar, float with 151 proof rum, and ignite.

4. Put out the flames and shoot.

What Alcohol Will Light on Fire?

The word *proof* comes from understanding what booze will light on fire. At room temperature, spirits over 100 proof will ignite. In old British navy days, spirits were stored with gunpowder. This not only kept the alcohol safe, but also ensured that the gunpowder would remain explosive even if the spirits spilled.

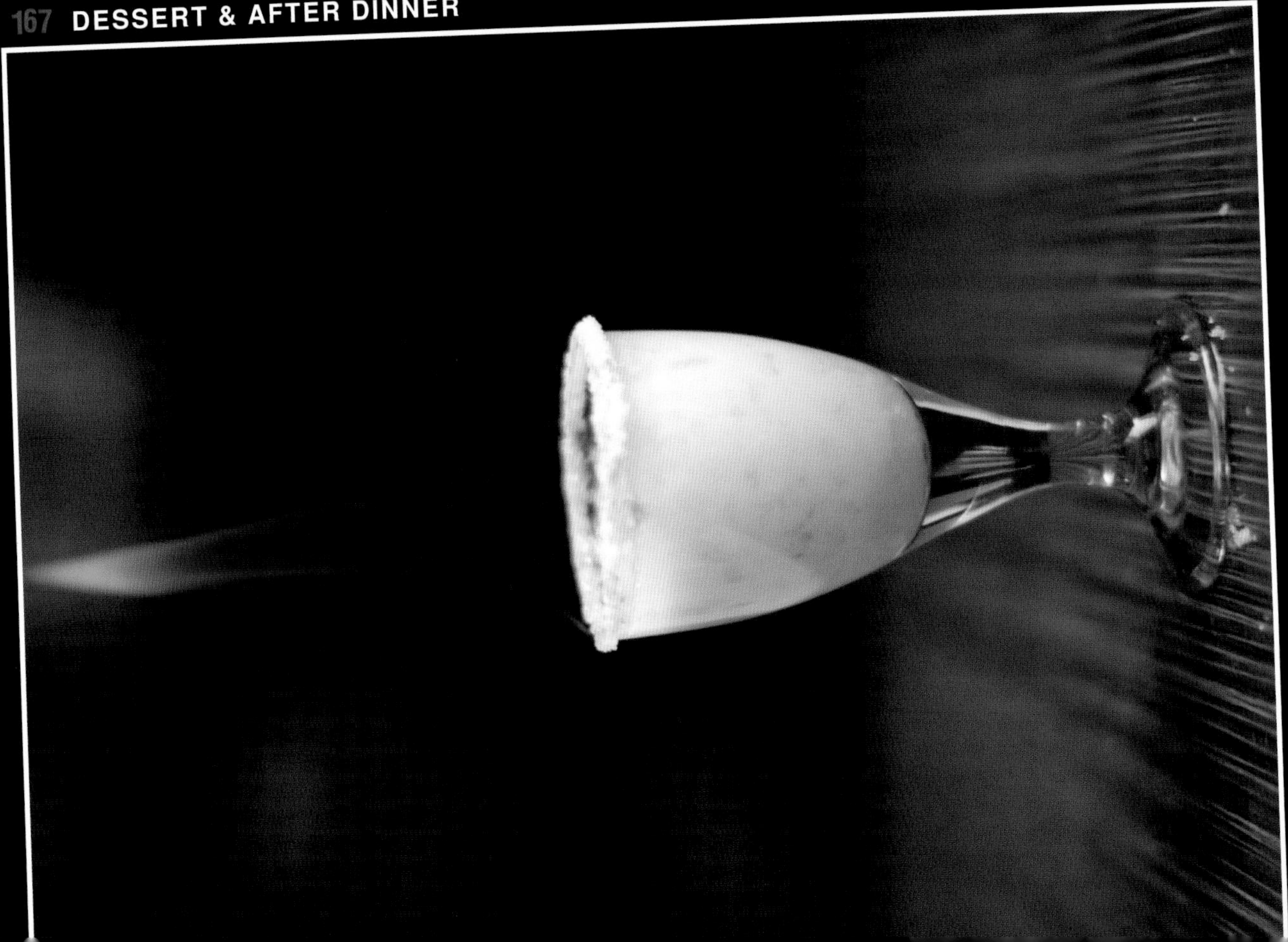

Matcha

Tea and whiskey are good friends. Unfortunately, green tea is considered healthy, so it's rarely mixed with alcohol. The Matcha shot doesn't actually have Matcha in it because it would be too expensive, but its flavor is simulated by using Japanese whiskey and just a touch of cream. The Japanese whiskey will add some sweetness and earthiness to this delicious shot.

MAKES

1 ounce very strong green tea

1 ounce Japanese whiskey

.25 ounce cream

1. Shake and strain into a shot glass.

Japanese Whiskey

Over 100 years ago, the Japanese people began making whiskey. This was mostly blended whiskey, but in the 1980s, they turned their hand to single malt whiskey. They are now recognized as making some of the best single malts in the world. These malts are made from Scottish malted barley but aged and distilled in Japan. Thus, they are Japanese single malt whiskey and Japanese blended whiskey, but not Scotch—which can only be made in Scotland.

Striped Biologist Taunter

If you recognize this as a joke from the TV show Futurama, *don't tell anyone because they'll know you are a nerd. If you don't already know, this stripy shot is named for a fictional mean animal with a target on its chest. This fictional animal went extinct for obvious reasons. This shot is indeed an explosion of flavor and is designed to be thrown down all in one gulp, at which point the drinker will experience flavors and smells on par with the fanciest chocolatier's truffle. The Striped Biologist Taunter is also a study on balancing sweetness. The shot's bottom two stripes are sweet and the top two are dry; it is very easy to adjust to suit your needs.*

MAKES

.25 ounce clear crème de cacao, chilled

.25 ounce Chambord, chilled

.75 ounce apricot eau-de-vie, chilled

.25 ounce violet liqueur, chilled

1. In order, slowly pour each ingredient into a shot glass.

Eau-de-Vie

Eau-de-vie means "water of life" in French. It refers to the un-aged distillate of just one flavor, normally a fruit. Therefore, apricot eau-de-vie would be just distilled apricots with no sugar and no flavors from wood or anything else. When made well, the result is a bone-dry, perfect flavor and aroma from whatever was distilled.

Pocket Pear

Generally speaking all desserts can be filed into two camps: Chocolate and Other. Chocolate is easy enough to define, but Other is pretty worthless unless there is good fruit. The clear choice for any dessert is one order of Chocolate and one order of Other. The idea of the Pocket Pear is to provide the best dessert possible in just one shot.

MAKES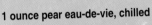

1 ounce pear eau-de-vie, chilled

.5 ounce crème de cacao, chilled

1. In order, slowly pour each chilled ingredient into a shot glass.

How Do They Get That Pear in a Bottle of Brandy?

Although it sounds pretty unrealistic, all you do is take a bottle and tie it to a blossom on a pear tree and let the pear grow in the bottle. If you try to explain this to the average person, you'll find it's like swearing that Santa is the Easter Bunny's arch-enemy, so you'll need other more plausible lies. Try something like "It is an optical illusion," or "it's actually a fake foam pear," to get more people to believe you.

Make Your Own Crème de Cacao

Crème de cacao is very easy to make at home if you'd like to have a nicer bottle. Steep cocoa nibs in dark rum for a week, strain the nibs, and then mix in one part rich simple syrup by volume. Rich syrup is just simple syrup that is two parts sugar to one part water.

Currant and Cask

Just because you see a layered shot doesn't mean that it is going to be sugar and everything nice; sometimes it will be spice and everything fierce. The Currant and Cask will taste like the most manly currant scone ever. And if you want to take it up a notch on the Chuck Norris meter, add a pat of butter to this one. The whiskey will balance out the sweet crème de cassis, but whiskey of this strength could balance a hurricane. The chocolate bitters are just a nice flavor note to finish on.

MAKES

.75 ounce crème de cassis, chilled

.25 ounce cask strength bourbon, chilled

2 dashes chocolate bitters, chilled

1. Gently pour each ingredient in order into a shot glass.

Cask Strength: *Beware!*

Cask strength refers to the alcoholic content of a spirit straight out of the barrel or "cask." Obviously the proof varies due to age and aging circumstances, but it is not unusual for cask strength spirits to have 50% more alcohol than their sissy filtered cousins. But therein lies the real danger: If the 50% more alcohol doesn't get you (and it will), then the unfiltered spirit will. Filtration removes impurities that cause hangovers.

Little Lebowski Urban Achiever

The B-52 was the quintessential pousse-café of the 1970s. This is a layered shot that many bartenders were taught to make in the cheesiest way possible: Pour these liquors slowly over a cherry and then offer the cherry to the guest. Perhaps the modern version of the B-52 can be the Little Lebowski Urban Achiever. Yes, this is essentially a White Russian but in shot form. Use caution though: The White Russian is actually a very dangerous cocktail for two reasons. It goes down smooth with a lot of alcohol and calories.

MAKES

.5 ounce Kahlúa, chilled

.5 ounce Baileys, chilled

.5 ounce vodka, chilled

1. In order, slowly pour each ingredient into a shot glass.

Vodka in the Freezer?

Of course you need a bottle of vodka in your freezer! What if some folks from the Russian embassy came over and you had nothing to serve them with caviar? Okay, so the chances of that happening are slim, but there are plenty of everyday reasons to keep vodka on hand—like when you're hanging a picture and hit your thumb with a hammer or lose your job. It's even great for the good times, like unexpected promotions and birthday celebrations. So the lesson here? Always keep a bottle of vodka in your freezer.

The Caracas

The Caracas is more a food preparation than it is a shot preparation. This shot uses Venezuelan rum, which is known to be complex without the sweetness of many other aged rums. The rest of the shot is a bizarre little snack. You'll need a razor-sharp knife to cut wafer-thin wheels of lime. Dip one half of the lime wheel in ground espresso and dip the other half of the lime wheel in very fine sugar. The next step is to eat that little black-and-white treat you just created. After a couple seconds of chewing or completely swallowing this citrus, you'll take the shot of Venezuelan rum. You'll feel a symphony of flavors take place that can't be described. This process is a signature shot from Jay Kuehner in Seattle's Sam Bar.

MAKES

1 lime wheel dipped in very fine
    sugar and ground espresso
1.5 ounces Venezuelan rum

1. Eat the lime wheel.
2. Shoot 1.5 ounces of Venezuelan rum.

Rums from Different Islands

Rum is not really strictly defined by appellation, but is stylistically defined by the country from where it comes. Puerto Rican rum is very light in flavor, rum from French-speaking nations is often blended like cognac, Jamaica's rum is sweet and spicy, and the rums of Central America are very dry. You should keep all of these things in mind in terms of what kind of cocktail you're trying to build.

The Extern

Perhaps you can call it a punishment shot. The Extern is a version of the classic pousse-café cocktail. Originally a seven-layer drink meant to be sipped after dinner one liqueur at a time, this shot became a tradition in culinary kitchens. Culinary students turning 21 years old would put one of these down on their birthday.

MAKES

.25 ounce grenadine, chilled

.25 ounce dark crème de cacao, chilled

.25 ounce maraschino liqueur, chilled

.25 ounce blue curaçao, chilled

.25 ounce Liquore Strega, chilled

.25 ounce Cointreau, chilled

.25 ounce dark rum, chilled

1. In order, slowly pour each ingredient into a shot glass.

Layering Liqueurs?

When layering spirits, the most important thing to start with is cold spirits. This increases their viscosity and makes them separate easier. Do not fret if things don't pour in perfect order. If the ingredients are cold enough, they will frequently separate on their own. In creating new pousse-cafés or substituting ingredients, take into account the sugar content more than the proof of the alcohol because sugar is heavier than higher-proof alcohol.

Cricket

Everyone knows this joke: A grasshopper walks into the bar and the bartender says, "Hey, you know we have a drink named for you?" and the grasshopper says, "You've got a drink named Irving?" The Grasshopper is a drink rarely ever ordered by human beings. It is best suited for leprechauns or to induce sleep. The Cricket, however, is a mature version of the Grasshopper using Fernet Branca as its base. It was created by Bryn Lumsden.

MAKES

.75 ounce Fernet Branca

.5 ounce cream

.5 ounce crème de cacao

1. Shake and strain into a glass.

Bitter + Sugar = Complex Flavors

If you heard that Fernet Branca tastes like peppermint gasoline, believe it. However, you can save this spirit by burying the intense flavor in cream, chocolate, and sugar. It not only suppresses the lovely notes of "fuel," but also allows the gentle mint and herb notes to shine through.

Homemade Crème de Cacao

Currently, there isn't really a good crème de cacao on the market. To make your own, soak equal parts cocoa nibs in a quality dark rum for one week. Then, strain this mixture. Combine what you have left with an equal part of rich syrup (2 parts sugar to 1 part water) and you'll have something better than anything you can buy.

Good Faith

Nobody actually likes the Rusty Nail. It is a cocktail that ruins Scotch by mixing it with another Scotch-based liqueur. However, everyone loves Baileys—should they choose to admit it or not. The Good Faith shot combines the guilty pleasure of Baileys with Irish Cream and adds Scotch and Drambuie for substance. The result is a sweet drink that you could put in a baby's bottle yet is so strong that any bearded lumberjack would enjoy it. Experiment with the ratios on this one to get the right amount of sweetness from Drambuie and Baileys, but remember that Drambuie is still 80 proof, so this shot packs a punch.

MAKES

.5 ounce Scotch

.5 ounce Baileys

.5 ounce Drambuie

1. Shake and strain into a glass.

Mixing Single Malt Scotches

There is no Scotch too viable not to mix with. However, many people choose Scotches that they have no business mixing into cocktails. Pick a single malt Scotch that is between ten and twelve years of age and stick to something Bayside or Lowland. If smokiness is what you desire, still use Bayside or Lowland, but add a dash of the smoky Scotch; you'll be shocked to see how far the flavor goes.

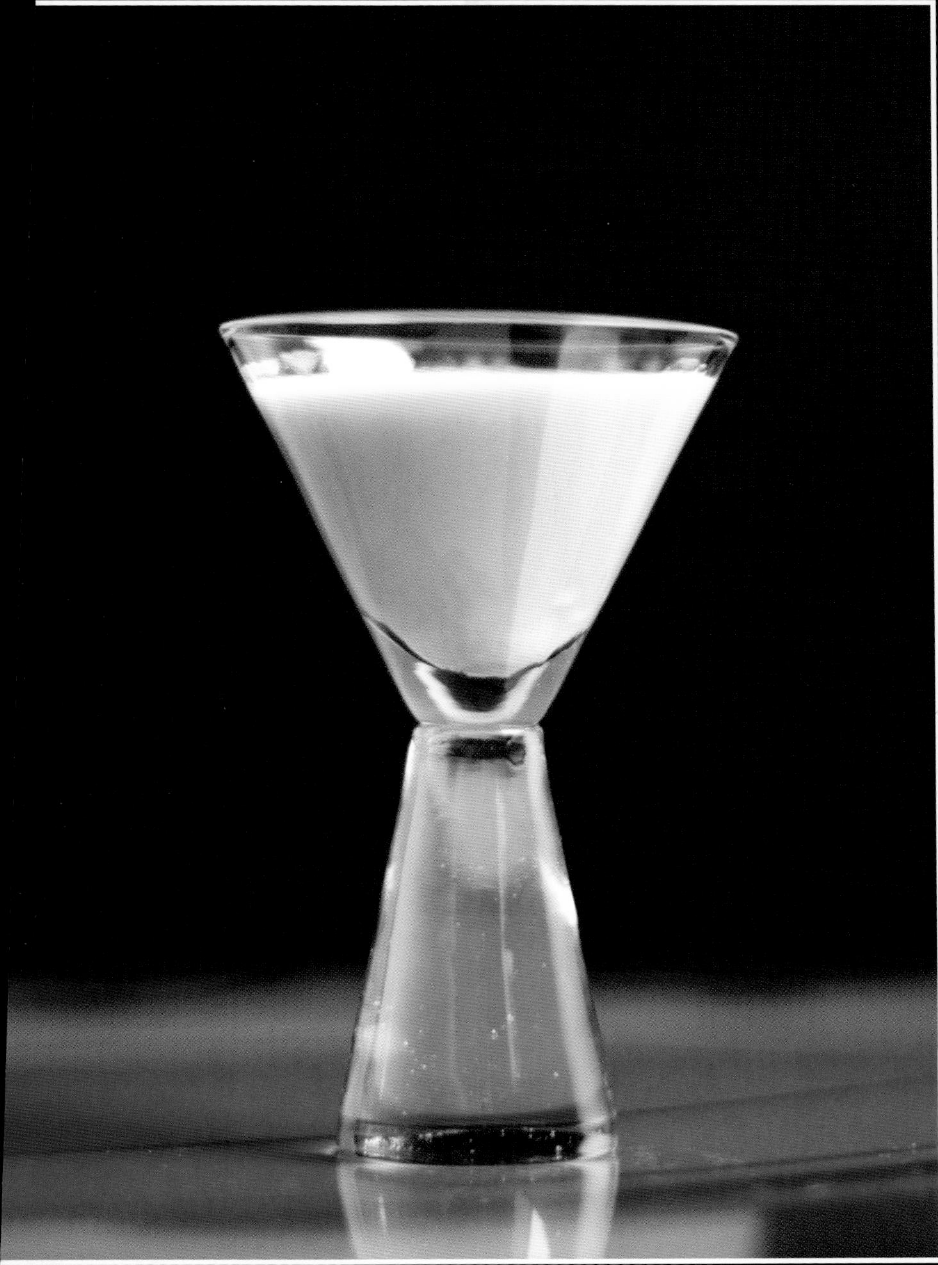

Salted Caramel Shot

It's the trendy flavor of ice cream and candy made into alcohol! Butterscotch brings the caramel flavor into this drink and bourbon provides the backbone.

MAKES

1 ounce bourbon

.5 ounce heavy cream

.25 ounce butterscotch liqueur

1 pinch kosher salt

1. Shake and strain into a shot glass.

Girls Just Want to Get Stinking Drunk

Except for being bereft of a bawdy name, the Salted Caramel Shot is a perfect cocktail to change mild-mannered bachelorette parties. With a few of these, a tame celebration turns into a wild night of dancing on bars and getting arrested.

Bitter Bike

Sometimes bitters really tie the drink together. When I first heard of the combination of St. Germain and Crème Yvette I felt like I was in for something that smelled like grandma and tasted of coffee syrup. This would be the case were it not for the addition of Angostura bitters atop this layered shot. Angostura dries the shot out, balances the aroma, and cleans the palate.

MAKES

1 ounce St. Germain, chilled

.25 Crème Yvette, chilled

4 dashes Angostura bitters, chilled

1. In order, slowly pour each ingredient into a shot glass.

St. Germain

St. Germain is an elderflower liqueur. Be sure not to confuse this with the elderberry; while it's from the same plant, the berry is an acidic funky fruit. Elderflowers are tiny yellow blossoms that are harvested all across Europe between two to four weeks of the year. If you see elderflower products on the shelf, they were likely harvested and produced that year. Elderflower is also considered an antiviral, so cheers to your health!

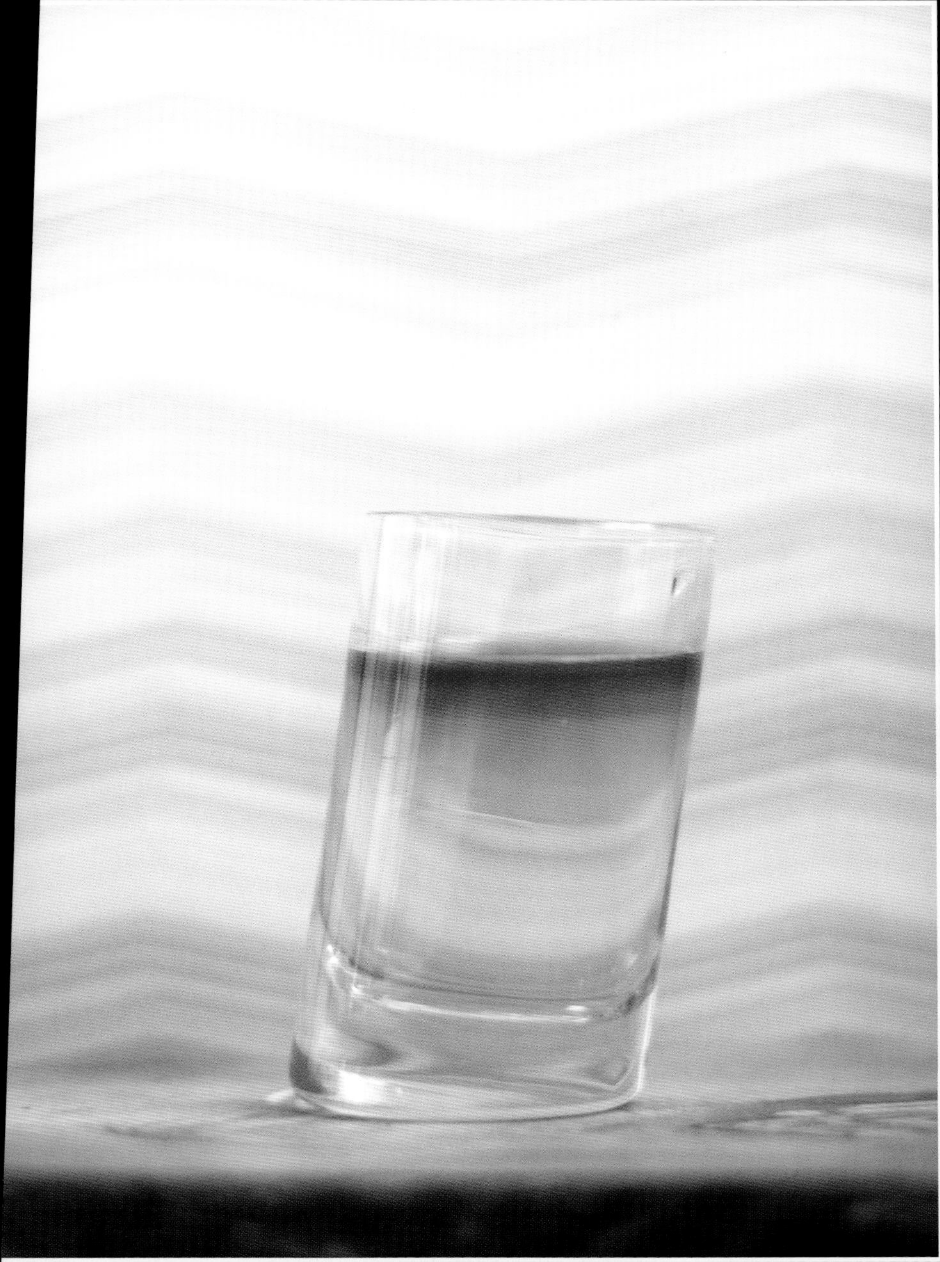

Midnight Water

The Midnight Water gets its name from being as dark as a black steer's butt on a moonless prairie night. The Midnight Water was invented by bartender Philip Trickey, who named it out of pure silliness. At the end of a long day it is much more fun to have an oats soda than a beer. There is a growing trend among bartenders for many cocktails to be "brown, bitter, and stirred." This trend could be brought to an end because the Midnight Water is clearly the winner in these tough-guy drinks.

MAKES

1 ounce bourbon

.25 ounce Averna

2 dashes Peychaud's bitters

1 dash simple syrup

1 orange zest

1. Stir and strain first four ingredients into a shot glass.
2. Garnish with a flamed orange zest.

Averna, Amaro, Amari: *What Does It All Mean?*

Amaro is a generic Italian term for a bitter after-dinner drink, *Amari* is the plural version of that word, and *Averna* is a brand name. If there is a town in Italy with two old men, that town will likely produce at least two types of Amari. These spirits are generally green based, infused with bitter herbs and spices, and then finished with caramelized sugar. Once you fall in love with amaro, you won't know how to finish a meal without it.

Strumpet

Actually this shot is more of a tart—ha, wordplay! But on the culinary side of things, the Strumpet shot is a little eggy delight that you can make from your pantry. And true to a tart it will have a whole egg in it. Though this might sound unusual at first, eggs in cocktails go way back. Shakespeare wrote of having a sack posset with a loved one, a custardy eggy potation. And let us not forget the humble nog, it goes back about 400 years as well. The Strumpet shot will also taste better if you use real vanilla extract rather than the fake vanilla flavoring, but that'll cost you extra.

MAKES

2 ounces Grand Marnier

1 whole egg

.5 ounce lemon juice

2 dashes vanilla extract

2 teaspoons powdered sugar

1. Shake first four ingredients very hard and fine strain into two shot glasses.
2. Garnish with powdered sugar.

Food Safety

Drinking raw eggs is pretty safe, but think of it like eating sushi: It is dangerous when you are stupid. To quote Anthony Bourdain, "You never go to the place with the sign that says, 'discount sushi.'" When you are eating raw, you need the finest ingredients and you need to keep them cold and fresh. After all, you wouldn't eat anything raw that was sitting in your fridge for a couple weeks, right? So use eggs that are only a couple days old. Lastly, most of the bad bacteria is on the eggshell, so crack eggs in a separate vessel to the one you are cooking or mixing with and always wash your hands.

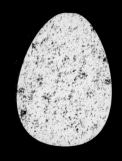

Witch's Tit

Witch's Tit is slightly classier than the name itself. It is a bartender tradition to name every cocktail with Liquore Strega in it for a witch. The very famous yellow bottle bears the visage of a witch, and tradition says that witches gather in the small town in Italy to imbibe this liqueur.

MAKES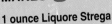

1 ounce Liquore Strega

.5 ounce vodka

.25 ounce cream

1. Shake and strain into a shot glass.

Liquore Strega

Liquore Strega is similar in flavor to yellow Chartreuse. It is flavored with herbs and spices—most notably saffron—and then aged for one year in a barrel. It is one of the few Italian liqueurs that bridges the gap between aperitivo and digestivo.

Woodsman

The flavors and smells of the woods are more appetizing than you would assume. And although it is difficult to believe, Douglas fir eau-de-vie is more enjoyable than it seems. However, it is as it sounds: distilled pine needles. If that sounds like a nightmare to you, consider that it is just a bottled flavor of Christmas. Alcohol made from pine trees and pinecones are traditional across northern Europe, though they do not show up in many classic cocktails.

MAKES

1 ounce pear juice

.5 Douglas fir eau-de-vie

.5 ounce vodka

1. Shake and strain into a shot glass.

Where Do I Find This Stuff?

HTTP://WWW.

When searching for more obscure booze to make shots like the Woodsman, remember that the Internet is your friend. Your state's liquor store may not have even heard of some of these alcohols, but the Internet is a great source. And the great states of California and New York are certainly interested in shipping them to you. Is it legal? It's no more illegal than doing a rolling stop in your car.

Funeral Shot

Sometimes you have to drink on a sad occasion. This is a very simple bittersweet drink created to commemorate the loss of a friend or family member—or less depressing, a canceled television show. The five stages of grief are in this shot and you can taste them all. Denial is on top: The shot smells of baked goods and tastes of good old, "nothing is wrong" vodka. Anger shows at the first taste of bitterness. Bargaining is the desire for that flavor to go away. Depression is the fact that it isn't going away. And acceptance is the sweet lingering finish.

MAKES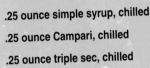

.25 ounce simple syrup, chilled

.25 ounce Campari, chilled

.25 ounce triple sec, chilled

.25 ounce vodka, chilled

1 dash Angostura bitters

1. In order, slowly pour each refrigerated ingredient into a shot glass.

Syrup: *The Easiest Way to Cheat for Layered Shots*

Crème liqueurs are at least 40% sugar, and most every syrup you'll make or find will be over 50% sugar. A dash of grenadine, simple syrup, orgeat, or anything that your barista uses to flavor your coffee can anchor any pousse-café. This dash of syrup will also leave a lingering finish of sweetness to a shot.

Part 6

SHOTS OF LAST RESORT

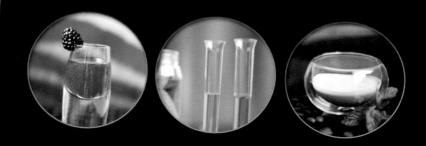

You have a jar of pickles, some amaretto, and a bottle of cooking sherry. What are you going to make? Well, with that list, one would just drink the amaretto straight, but in this chapter we'll go over how to make shots in the real world. Many of us don't have an immaculately stocked home bar, but we do have stray bottles of whatnot, more types of jelly than anyone would ever need, and that ubiquitous pickle jar. It might be surprising, but that is enough to still make some shots—and not just punishment shots. Most anybody's house has enough fixins to chef up great treats—simply remember that creativity and bravery are a must. Let's take some chances!

Lil Ni

In the world of alcohol, ni always means vinegar. The Lil Ni is an odd cocktail that uses that white wine vinegar for something quite valuable. When you muddle a little bit of lemon peel with vinegar and simple syrup, you begin to make a small lemon gastrique. You can use this gastrique on its own as a garnish on a plate—but if you add gin, you create a great cocktail. The acidity from vinegar makes this an incredibly refreshing shot and cleanses your palate, which gets you ready to have another.

MAKES

.25 ounce simple syrup

1 ounce gin

.25 ounce white vinegar

1 swath lemon peel

1. Muddle ingredients together.
2. Shake and strain into a shot glass.

Drinking Vinegar

There are urban legends about drinking a pint of vinegar to pass a drug test. However, that is only something your enemy would tell you. Regular old white wine vinegar doesn't show up in many drinks, but throughout Southeast Asia, more palatable "drinking vinegars" are actually quite common. These high-acidity beverages are an esoteric soft drink and are great for making cocktails.

La Padrina

For some reason, it seems that everyone has a bottle of amaretto lying around the house. Rental properties normally come with the half-drunk model left somewhere in the house by someone who couldn't stand to move the bottle again. Amaretto is actually quite useful because it mixes with almost everything. La Padrina is a play on the Godmother cocktail. The Godmother blends vodka, amaretto, and cream, and is generally acceptable. However, La Padrina will be more like a Creamsicle with the addition of tequila and orange juice.

MAKES

1 ounce tequila

.25 ounce orange juice

.25 ounce cream

.5 ounce amaretto

1. Shake and strain into a shot glass.

Freshly Squeezed Juice

Don't think about citrus juice in ounces; think about them in cocktails. The average full-size cocktail will require the juice from one lime, one half of a lemon, one half of an orange, or one quarter of a grapefruit. Think about this when shopping for cocktail ingredients.

Baby Bradsell

Dick Bradsell is a famous London barman best known for inventing the Bramble, and it is clear that Dick's surname is much better suited for naming drinks. The Bramble is basically a gin sour using blackberry liqueur to add fruity freshness. As an homage to the Bramble, the Baby Bradsell will use blackberry jam to give you all the sugar and fruit you need. Think of the Baby Bradsell in winter months or early spring when, as the British would say, "Fruit and veg are a bit crap."

MAKES

1 ounce gin

.5 ounce blackberry jam

.25 ounce lemon juice

1. Shake and strain into a shot glass.

Blackberries: *The Summertime Ingredient*

Depending on where you live, blackberry season is from late spring through summer. In the winter, do not buy blackberries that taste of cardboard. Blackberries are best when picked by small hands for free. Specifically, use Tom Sawyer's logic and get some kid to do it for you. Try this technique: "Hey (insert name of niece, nephew, or offspring), I bet you can't fill this bowl with blackberries!"

Fernet and Figs

The Fernet and Figs shot is a great way to get through the holiday season's left-over fig jam and truly confuse the palates of your friends and family. There are certain sweet-and-sour notes only recognized when in Newton form that blend so well with minty herbal tones from Fernet. But unless you are trying to create a shot that tastes of bizarre mouthwash, be sure to add a touch of simple syrup.

MAKES

1 ounce Fernet Branca

1 ounce fig jam

.5 ounce simple syrup

1. Shake and strain into a shot glass.

Jams and Jellies in Cocktails

Every jam and every jelly in your fridge is a time capsule for fresh fruits. Remember? They are called *preserves* for a reason. You can add any jelly to a cocktail to bring forth an amazing fruity note. In many cases, jams and jellies work better than using fresh fruits (unless you are picking at the height of the season). Just remember that you'll need to strain these shots and cocktails.

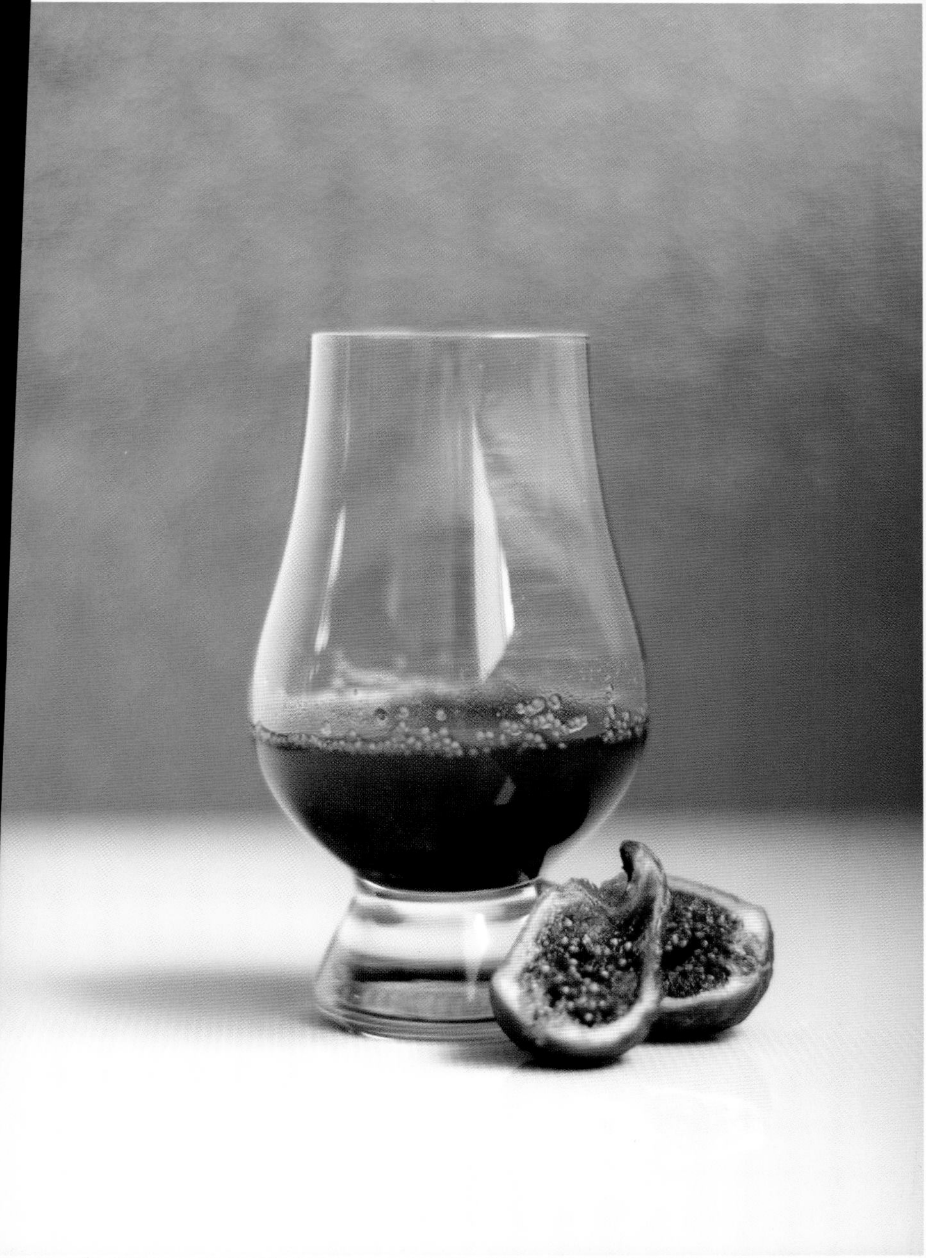

L'Orange

Ask chefs how they feel about MSG and they'll tell you it truly is the flavor enhancer. The L'Orange is a little bastardized way to get drunk off the sweet and sour sauce packet from your favorite Chinese restaurant. Basically, this is the Chinese takeout equivalent of a Sidecar. Instead of adding lemon and orange, you're including a lemon-flavored sauce that adds some sort of amazing sweetness. This cocktail may never take off past the average college dorm, but it will always be useful in a pinch—especially if no one watches you make it.

MAKES

1 ounce brandy

1 packet sweet and sour sauce

1. Shake and strain into a shot glass.

Fast-Food Condiments

Making cocktails with condiment ingredients from takeout orders and your favorite fast-food place is not as insane as it sounds. These little foil-wrapped gems are amazingly well made to balance sweetness with salt, savory, and acidity. A common way to add sugar to a savory dish is to just use ketchup. Need salt flavor? Try adding soy sauce, a handy trick to use in the kitchen.

Tequila'd Pickle Juice

Taking an ice cold shot of vodka and chasing it with a bite of pickle or caviar is a Russian tradition. It is difficult to attribute the Pickle-back cocktail to Brooklyn, New York, but it is a genius way to not waste pickle brine. The Pickle-back is exactly as it sounds: a shot of whiskey with a pickle brine chaser. The Tequila'd Pickle Juice is the same thing, but now with flavors more like the contents of a bachelor's fridge. The salty acidity from the pickle brine gets you ready to immediately have that next shot of whisky again. Or perhaps the pickle brine gets you ready to go to your favorite deli and have a Reuben.

MAKES

1 ounce reposado tequila

1 ounce pickle brine

1. Shoot the tequila at room temperature and chase it with a frosty right-out-of-the-fridge shot of pickle juice.

Pickle Juice, Olive Juice, Pickle Brine: What Are These Things?

You cannot get olive juice and pickle brine simply by squeezing olives and pickles until their juice comes out. These little devils are basically soaking in salt water and vinegar. The essence of a Dirty Martini is basically the desire to add the balance of salt and acidity to a cocktail.

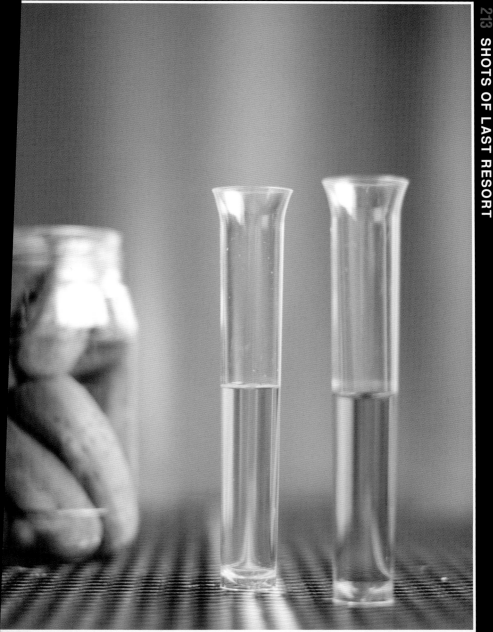

Custard Shot

Two words: Mango Lassi. If you've been to an Indian restaurant, then you obviously know that drinking yogurt is amazing. Chances are, your refrigerator is full of yogurt you don't exactly like because the road to hell is paved with good intentions. The Custard Shot uses your yogurt and, well, whatever else you have around the house, to create a generally healthy libation. It isn't often that you get to have a shot that has protein, vitamin C, and living cultures in it to help your digestion. Use fruit-on-the-bottom yogurt for a difficult yet rewarding shot.

MAKES

1 ounce yogurt

1 ounce rum

.5 ounce simple syrup

1. Shake and strain into a shot glass.

A Sprinkle of This and a Sprinkle of That

It's time to raid your spice rack. Think about flavor pairings for this Custard Shot. Strawberry yogurt? Perhaps a pinch of black pepper. Mango yogurt? Maybe a touch of cardamom. For each cup of yogurt a grocery store has to offer, your spice rack has a way to enhance it.

Chard-o-jar

Most people who have white wine around the house don't have a hard time getting through it. However, if a bottle is left unattended it will still go bad in the fridge. When white wine oxidizes it generally becomes more acidic. The good news? This added acidity makes it perfect to mix with alcohol. If you don't have any old white wine floating around your house, try using sauvignon blanc or unoaked chardonnay.

MAKES

1 ounce white wine

.5 ounce St. Germain

2 dashes celery bitters

1. Shake and strain into a shot glass.

Elderflower Liqueur

Maybe it's that elderflower tastes like lychee, which intrigues us, but what elderflower really does to cocktails is a certain something that makes us want more. Elderflower is indeed the biggest flavor trend of the past ten years, and deservedly so. The ingredient itself goes back hundreds of years in Europe, and its magic balance of floral notes and acidity on the palate mean it can be added to almost anything.

Inebriatti

The average person collects salad dressing at a rate of two bottles per year every year after college. Unless you live a very healthy lifestyle, you likely have more salad dressing than you know what to do with. The good news is that many of these salad dressings are vinegar-based and can be mixed with alcohol to make very interesting shots. Unfortunately, your ranch dressing is just going to have to stay in the fridge until the next time you make buffalo wings.

MAKES

.5 ounce Italian salad dressing

1 ounce grappa

.5 ounce water

1. Shake and strain into a shot glass.

Secret Herbal Recipes

Hundreds of years ago, monks and alchemists began combining spirits with sugars, herbs, and spices to make what were in effect secret elixirs for health. One could not exactly say that the manufacturers of salad dressings are trying to re-create these secret elixirs, but they do use the same herbs and spices to make their recipes today. Things like anise, mace, rosemary, and oregano are all ingredients that show up in both liqueurs and salad dressings. Perhaps these two bizarre liquids are not too far away from each other after all.

Vieux Rouge

Do you ever look at your spice rack and think, "Where did this even come from?" As discussed earlier at great length, shots are best made in sets. You can make your own prebottled cocktail just by using your spice rack, a bottle of wine, and a touch of brandy.

MAKES

1 bottle red wine

1 cup sugar

2 cinnamon sticks or 1 teaspoon ground

10 cloves or 1 teaspoon ground

1 pinch black pepper

1 pinch cayenne pepper

1 pinch "other" (make it your own!)

6 ounces brandy

1. Place first seven ingredients in a saucepan and bring to a boil.
2. Stir while boiling for 10 minutes.
3. Remove from heat and add brandy.
4. Fine strain and allow to chill in the fridge.
5. Pour 1.5 ounces into a shot glass and serve.

Liqueurs: How Are They Made?

One of the main ways liqueurs are made is by pouring hot wine and spirits over herbs and spices. This process is called *percolation*. That is exactly what you'll be doing here. It's absolutely fine to make your own liqueur so long as you don't sell it. If moonshining is a goal of yours, you can start your life of crime here.

Mall Santa

An old man with a beard who speaks loudly in the third person is clearly drunk. However, society allows these people to wear a red suit and work with children. The Mall Santa shot is a great way to cope with holiday stress and deal with left-over coffee. It is also a bizarre universal truth that most households have a bottle of peppermint schnapps.

MAKES

1 ounce cold coffee

.5 ounce peppermint schnapps

.5 ounce cream

1. Shake and strain into a shot glass.

Finally—A Use for Instant Coffee

The best coffee you can use for cocktails is a cold brew. If you live by a trendy urban coffee shop, buy some there. For everybody else, it's corner-cutting time: Just mix instant coffee with cold water for each shot. Never wait for old coffee to chill because it'll be too acidic. If you're looking for authenticity though, make this drink with old truck stop coffee and powdered nondairy creamer.

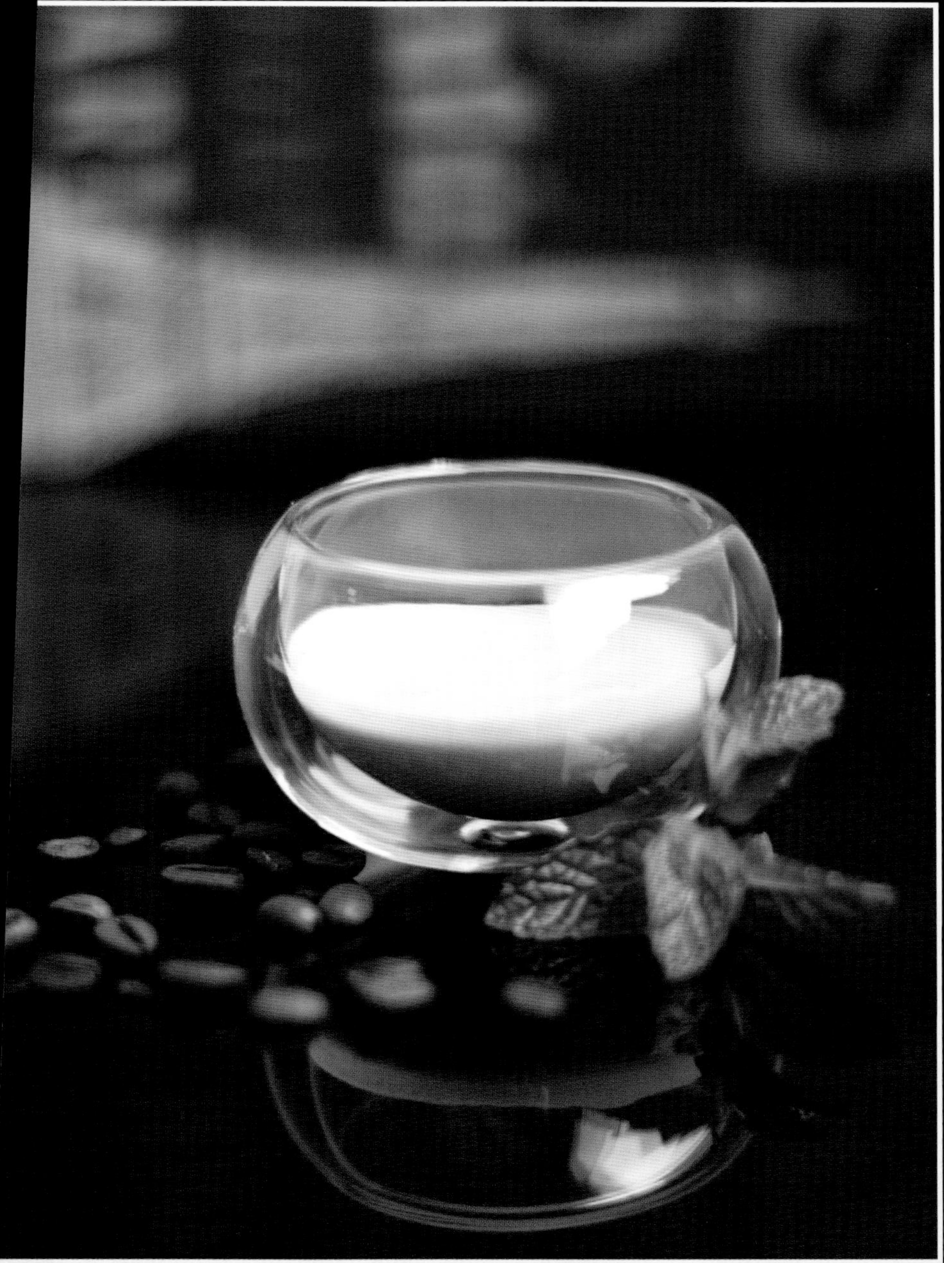

Afternoon Delight

It is a fool's game to buy prebottled sweet tea vodka. Leftover tea is something that you carry from kitchen to kitchen your entire life and you never drink it. However, Earl Grey tea is great because it has a beautiful orange note that pairs well with any spirit. The Afternoon Delight shot will use vodka to allow this bitter orange to shine through. You should enjoy this tea with an added touch of sugar and lemon to balance out the bitterness. And to really have fun, set up a little tea party with all your favorite stuffed animals!

MAKES

.5 ounce Earl Grey tea

1 ounce vodka

.25 ounce lemon juice

.25 ounce simple syrup

1. Shake and strain into a shot glass.

Tea-Infused Spirits

You may leave tea in a jar for a day to get a nice brew, but if you infuse a bottle of wine with it, it will take only a couple of hours. If you're looking for a quick fix, try infusing teabags into a bottle of booze; you'll only need five minutes since anything more would be far too bitter and tannic. Keep this easy technique in mind when making tea cocktails and tea shots at home.

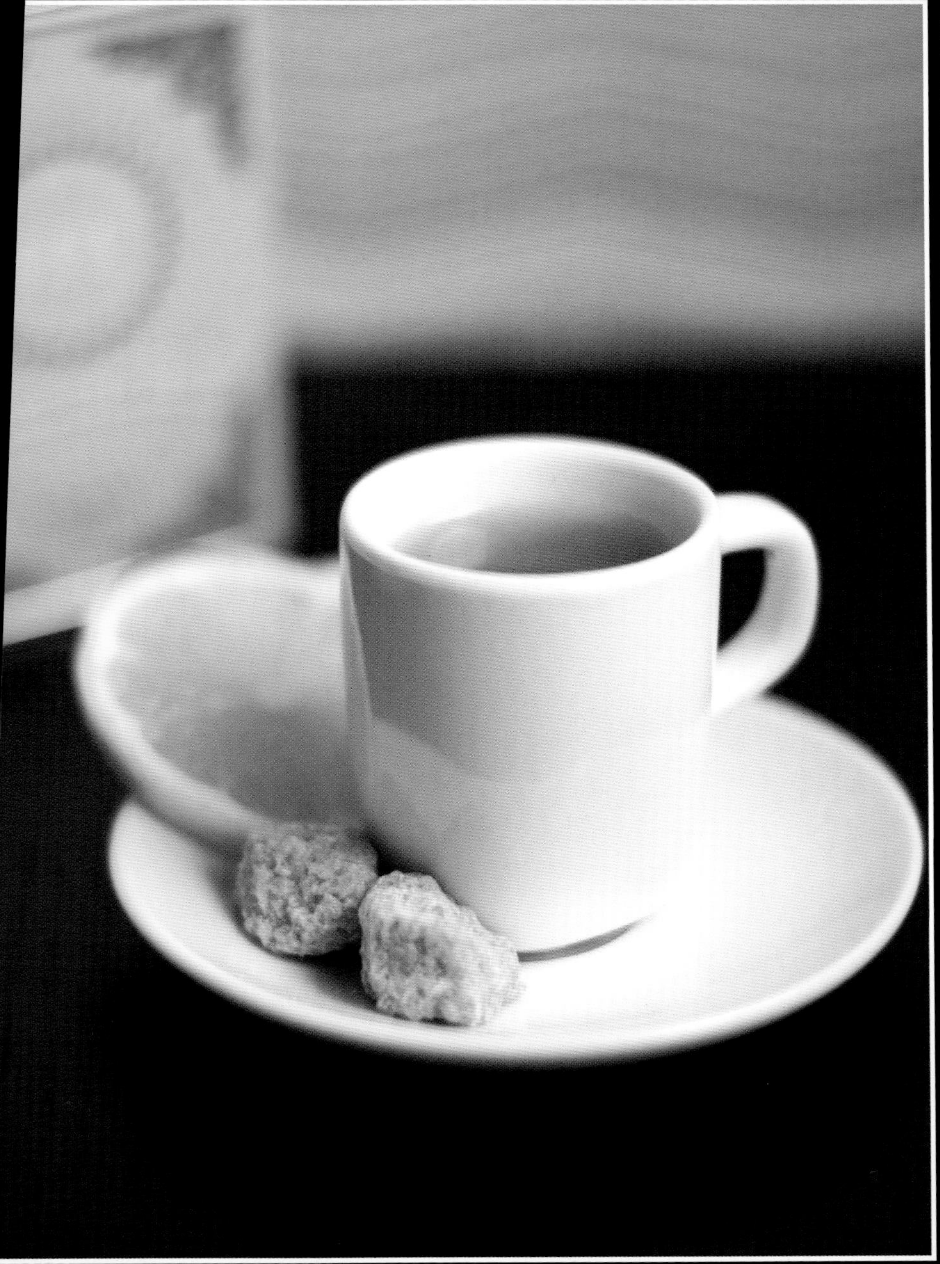

Sleepy Time

It is okay to use alcohol for medicinal reasons. It's actually one of the best ways to use alcohol. To maintain cultural relevance, the tea industry has brought up tea's many health benefits too. And while you'll frequently hear about people who get addicted to sleeping pills, you never hear about people who get addicted to Sleepy Time tea. If you take a cursory glance around the Internet and read through random boxes in the home, you'll notice that most Sleepy Time tea is a lovely blend of chamomile. Chamomile has a terrific balance for cocktails, and when you mix it with a bit of lime cordial, it makes for a great nighttime sleep aid.

MAKES

1 ounce rum

.5 ounce chamomile tea

.5 ounce lime cordial

1. Shake and strain into a shot glass.

Rum and Tea

Almost all traditional punch recipes have an element of tea and a base of gin or rum. The spices and botanicals in gin come from the world over and many ports in Indonesia carry rum's main ingredient (sugar cane). The actual herbal blend in chamomile or Sleepy Time tea are spices that would have grown next to the original sugar-cane fields in Indonesia. These products would have traveled the world together and were eventually mixed into punches long before cocktails and Sleepy Time tea ever existed.

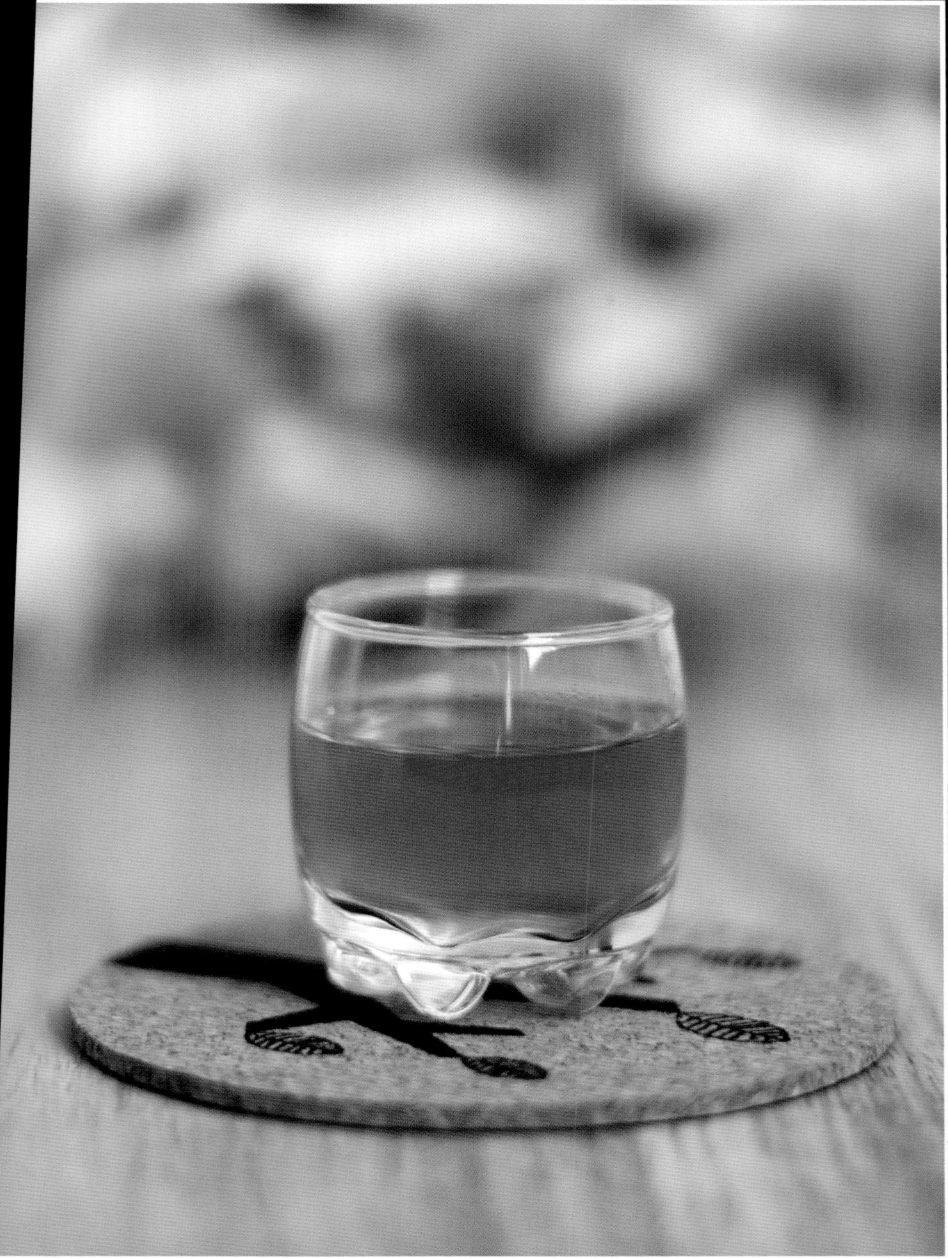

Lumberjack

The best thing about making drinks with maple syrup is that the maple syrup is already cold right out of the refrigerator. The worst thing about making shots with maple syrup is that you start to wonder why you don't always add liquor to your maple syrup. The Lumberjack shot seems like the perfect drink for men who work very hard all day in the outdoors and need a sweet kick at the end of the day. Or if you prefer the Monty Python version, it's for those who wear women's clothing and hang around in bars. Either way, it's a delicious answer to drinking with household ingredients.

MAKES

.25 ounce grade A maple syrup

1 ounce whiskey

2 dashes Angostura bitters

1. Shake and strain into a shot glass

How Important Is Grade A Maple Syrup?

When cooking, you should use the best maple syrup possible, but grade A maple syrup costs roughly as much as an eighteen-year-old bottle of Scotch. While it is an excellent choice to drink an eighteen-year-old Scotch, it doesn't always shine through in shots and the same can be said of maple syrup. Something from the grocery store will generally substitute fine for cocktails. But don't dare try to pull that kind of mess in Canada.

Lazy Sangrita

The stray bottle of tequila is another common household fixture. Tequila shots are a perfectly legitimate thing to do with one's time, but they are better enjoyed with a palate cleanser in between. Traditionally, this would've been a red blended beverage called Sangrita. The original Sangrita may have been no more than grenadine and orange juice, but modern versions are normally tomato and orange based. This high-acidity sipper is a great way to cleanse the palate between sips of tequila or to chase shots of less-than-perfect tequila.

MAKES

2 ounces mild salsa

2 ounces orange juice

4 dashes hot sauce

1 pinch black pepper

2-ounce shot of tequila

1. Blend first four ingredients together.
2. Sip with a 2-ounce shot of tequila.
3. Makes enough for 4 shots.

Legit Sangrita

Sangrita was probably always made in a lazy way. Some historians suggest that the original was nothing more than grenadine. However, to step up the Lazy Sangrita, you can replace the store-bought salsa with 4 tomatillos, 1/4 cup diced red onion, a sprig of cilantro, and a pinch of salt. The result is a vibrant Sangrita that also doubles as an amazing taco sauce.

INDEX

ABOUT THE AUTHOR

Andrew's father told him to be a *Playboy* photographer by day and a jazz musician by night. At the age of four, Andrew trusted his father's aspirations to be a mandate—he remains an acceptable photographer and a champion of the smoking jacket. He also snuck past the velvet rope with his trombone while underage, but found himself a better drink slinger than bop player. This began a questionable habit that spiraled into a suspect career behind the bar.

Andrew would hate to believe that drinking and serving whiskey eclipsed playing trombone, but this is somewhat true. Now, he just forces people to listen to J. J. Johnson while he crafts classic drinks and builds tomorrow's. His father deals with it.

Andrew dipsographs in a surly fashion at *www.cask strength.wordpress.com.* He is a cofounder and secretary of the Washington State Bartender's Guild. Andrew was a former bartender at Vessel and Rob Roy and the opening bar manager at both Naga Cocktail Lounge and Mistral Kitchen—all listed in *Food and Wine*'s top 100 bars in the world. He is currently a bartending ronin for hire, a mixology consultant, and the spirit director for Vinum Importing. He can also open a bottle of beer faster than any mortal.

the hungry Editor

Foodies Unite!

Bring your appetite and follow The Hungry Editor who really loves to eat. She'll be discussing (and drooling over) all things low-fat and full-fat, local and fresh, canned and frozen, highbrow and lowbrow. . .

When it comes to good eats, The Hungry Editor (and her tastebuds) do not discriminate!

It's a Feeding Frenzy—dig in!

Sign up for our newsletter at

www.adamsmedia.com/blog/cooking

and download our free **Top Ten Gourmet Meals for $7** recipes!